THEOLOGY
IN RABBINIC
STORIES

THEOLOGY
IN RABBINIC
STORIES

CHAIM PEARL

HENDRICKSON
PUBLISHERS

Hendrickson Publishers, Inc.
P. O. Box 3473
Peabody, Massachusetts 01961–3473

ISBN 1–56563–285–0

First Printing — November 1997

THEOLOGY IN RABBINIC STORIES, by Chaim Pearl
© 1997 Carta. The Israel Map and Publishing Company Ltd.,
P. O. Box 2500, Jerusalem.

Hendrickson Publishers' edition published by arrangement with Carta.
Printed in the United States of America

Table of Contents

Introduction

Rabbinic literature is divided into two chief parts, called *halakhah* and *aggadah*. The first is the legal discussion and decisions; the second comprises all the rest. In this volume we are concerned with the second part, the *aggadah*.

The word *aggadah* is the Aramaic equivalent of the Hebrew word *haggadah* which comes from the root "to tell" or "to relate" as in the term Passover Haggadah which is the book containing the narration of the story of the Exodus.

Since it refers to the entire corpus of non-legalistic rabbinic literature, the *aggadah* is a very comprehensive collection of writings. First of all, it includes the legends of the Jews which derive from rabbinic expositions of the Bible and their elaborations of the biblical story which provide an imaginative literary extension of the Bible narrative. Then there is a vast amount of *aggadah* which relates to events which took place and to personalities who lived after the biblical period. Because of the relative paucity of source material for this period of Jewish history, the aggadic accounts are especially valuable. Thirdly, there is a voluminous literature which recalls the stories and parables of the sages who lived from about 200 B.C.E. until the close of the Babylonian Talmud in 500 C.E. To this one can add some stories of the later leaders of Babylonian Jewry and their academies. Then there is the folklore which has no thematic connection with the Bible story or with famous personalities in the post-biblical period. Such folklore may deal with angels, with demons, or with quaint customs prevalent in some sections of the Jewish community. And finally, there are numerous philosophical and theological teachings which are included in the *aggadah*. Sometimes, these latter teachings are explicit in the story and then there is no difficulty at all in identifying and explaining them. This applies particularly in the area of ethics. For example, the talmudic collection popularly known as *Pirke Avot*, "The Ethics (or Sayings) of the Fathers" contains a number of generally clear teachings touching on the concepts of God, Man, Israel, Torah and the ethical life, all expressed in a fairly lucid and popular style. But very often the same teachings are taught by a parable and then the story has to be explored to deduce the lesson which the author has not made explicit. Of course, the stories are usually interesting enough on their own and are superb examples of the ancient parable. Yet, like Aesop's fables, they all have something to teach. The collection assembled in this book, for the most part, belongs to this genre of aggadic literature.

In reading these stories the reader always has to bear in mind that he is not dealing with history. That is to say, the story is not necessarily the record of what actually happened. Of course, a story may be historical or have its source in an historical event which actually happened. But for the most part the stories recorded here are not to be read as historical reports. However, there are different levels of truth. There is historical truth and moral truth. When the latter kind of truth is hidden in the story, it then becomes important always to ask, "Why did the rabbis tell this story? What does it teach?" A simple example of this will illustrate the point. Hanina ben Dosa was so poor that he acceded to his wife's plea and prayed that God send them some reward which they could use in this life and in this world, instead of having to wait for all their reward in the World to Come. So God sent down a golden leg of a golden table and the pious couple were over-joyed that their earthly poverty was ended. But their joy was short lived since Hanina had a dream that night that they were already in Paradise where he and his wife felt very embarrassed to be the only ones sitting at a table which wobbled on two legs. So next morning he prayed that God take back His gift. And miraculously that is what happened. History? Certainly not. Childish nonsense? Again, certainly not: the rabbis were not so naive. Then what is the purpose of the story? That is the question we have to ask of every piece of rabbinic legend. In this case the story is open to a variety of interpretations. In the first place it illustrates the rabbinic doctrine that there is life after death. Again, that there is reward and punishment. Further, that reward and punishment comes in the World to Come. Then it can teach that in life we are frequently called upon to reject the immediate pleasure for the sake of a greater but more remote value in the future. Every reader will find the best meaning for himself. And it is that kind of search for meaning which often makes the rabbinic legend more than just a good story. Folklore can also serve as a good moral guide in life.

A great deal has been written about the inter-relationship between *aggadah* and *halakhah*. Although this subject is outside the scope of this brief introduction, it is worth pointing out that there is a very significant fusion which really invalidates the strict separation of the two. While the rabbis wisely refused to base laws on aggadic folklore, miracle stories and legends, the ethical teachings of *aggadah* frequently inform and influence the spirit of the legal *halakhah*, so that the law then becomes more sensitive to the human situation. In an important essay on this theme, the great poet and scholar Hayyim Nahman Bialik pointed out that *aggadah* is a refinement of *halakhah*, while the *halakhah* is the codification of the essence of the *aggadah*. In other words, *aggadah* has made the law more ethical and *halakhah* has made the ethics obligatory.

In spite of what has just been said, efforts were made in special anthologies to separate the *aggadah* from the *halakhah*. The most noteworthy and successful work in this field was carried out by the fifteenth century scholar Jacob Ibn Habib (Salonica), who recognized the wide popularity of the *aggadah* for the masses of the people. He therefore took out all the *aggadah* from the Talmud and put it into a single large volume entitled *Ein Yaakov* which for very many years was a popular text in synagogues and study circles throughout the world. It has been published in well over one hundred editions, many of them with commentaries. Among the modern anthologies of rabbinic *aggadah* perhaps the best and the most popular is the collection known as *Sefer Ha-Aggadah*, compiled by Bialik and Rawnitzky, first published in 1910. These two great scholars not only translated much of the Aramaic into Hebrew, adding footnotes for difficult words and phrases, but they excelled in their judicious selection of the vast material. An English edition of part of this work has appeared, published by D'Vir (Tel Aviv). It so far includes the first two volumes of this encyclopedic work which I selected, translated and annotated.*

---

* More recently a literal English translation of the entire work by W. Broide was published by Schocken (New York).

The *aggadah* of the classical rabbinic period is found in two main sources, the Talmud and the Midrash. The Talmud is the great corpus of rabbinic discussion and codification which covers the period 200 B.C.E. until 500 C.E.

Now every student of the Talmud knows that interspersed in the legal discussions of the rabbis there are numerous elements of *aggadah*. In fact a considerable part of the Talmud is *aggadah*. Side by side with talmudic legal argument and exposition we read pieces about history, philosophy, theology, ethics and folklore. The Talmud is thus the first major source for *aggadah* and many of the stories which are included in this volume come from the Talmud.

The second classical storehouse for *aggadah* is the Midrash, a word which comes from the Hebrew *darash*, "to explain" or "to enquire." The Midrash is a collection of works written at different times and in different countries. Much of it offers expositions of the biblical books, sometimes on nearly every verse of a chapter. Although there are some midrashic works which deal with the legal aspects of Judaism, most of them are aggadic and provide a primary source for rabbinic folklore. The chief midrashim are the earliest which were written mostly in Eretz Israel, in the first centuries of the era, but were not edited until about 500 C.E. In this group there is the collection known as *Midrash Rabbah* (The Great Midrash) on the Pentateuch and the Five Scrolls, and from which a good part of our story collection has been selected. However, there are midrashim which were edited as late as the thirteenth or even the fourteenth centuries. In the thirteenth century two important anthologies of Midrash were written. One was the *Yalkut Shimoni* on the Bible, written in Europe, and the other was *Midrash Hagadol* on the Pentateuch, probably written in Yemen or Tiberias.

It will not come as a surprise therefore to learn that a literature which developed over a period of more than one thousand years and which was written in different countries should bear evidence of varied influences. Not only in the language—Greek words in the Palestinian midrashim and Persian words in the Babylonian midrashim—but also in the philosophical ideas expressed in the different books. In dealing with the theological and philosophical ideas of *aggadah* it is important to remember that much of it was written in the periods of Hellenistic-Roman civilization when Judaism was confronted by strong cultural cross-currents. When we discover some of those influences in the *aggadah* it becomes necessary to distinguish what is authentic rabbinic thought which subsequently entered into the mainstream of Jewish teaching, from what might be regarded as the temporary product of Babylonian, Greek or other external environmental influences.

This book concentrates on the main themes of theological and ethical interest and it is hoped that the stories and their expositions will help us to understand some central ideas in rabbinic thought. The presentation of the stories is not a translation of the original but has been specially written for this volume in a manner which, while it is absolutely faithful to its source, is offered in a free style which is easier for the modern reader. Finally, the author readily admits a certain subjective preference, both in his choice of stories and in his interpretations. This is inevitable in a work of this kind. Proper consideration has of course been given to the commentaries, both classical and modern, but in the final analysis the conclusions are influenced by the author's approach to Judaism which he believes has always been subject to historical development and to a Judaism which appeals to reason.

BEGINNINGS

1

~

Who Created the World?

One day a heathen approached Rabbi Akiba and asked him, "Who created the world?"

"God created the world" answered the rabbi.

"What proof do you have?" asked the man.

"Come back tomorrow" said Akiba "and I will give you some proof."

When the man returned the next day, Akiba said to him, "That's a nice coat you are wearing. I wonder who made it!"

"Why, the tailor made it of course" replied the man.

"What proof have you got that a tailor made it?" asked Akiba.

"What sort of question is that? Everyone knows that a tailor makes clothes!"

"In the same way" returned Akiba, "you can now understand that God created the world."

After the non-believer had left, Akiba elaborated a little further on the theme and said to his disciples, "Just as the existence of a house points to a builder who built it, and the clothes point to a tailor who sewed it, and the furniture to a carpenter who made it, so the existence of the world is proof in itself of an Almighty God who created it" (*Mid. Tem.*).

*   *   *

This brief anecdote illustrates one of the themes on the subject of the creation of the world as treated in rabbinic literature. Until the Greek and Roman periods it is hardly likely that Jewish thought was concerned with the metaphysical problems of the existence of God and the creation of matter. But with their exposure to Greek culture, Jewish teachers had to confront many philosophical and theological problems which gave their predecessors little or no concern.

Now for the believing Jew, the very first verse in the Bible gives the clear answer, *In the beginning God created the heavens and the earth* (Gen. 1:1). This verse makes two basic theological statements. First, in the beginning there was God. Second, out of that void God created everything that subsequently came into existence. For early Judaism the Bible statement was enough, and the believer was not overly troubled by any serious questions or doubts. The biblical verses succinctly answered the whole question.

But the Greek philosophers advanced other theories which attempted to explain the origin of matter without positing the notion of a divine creator. For the talmudic rabbis however, it was a simple matter of faith based on their reading of the Bible. At first there was nothing, only God. Then at a point in time and in accordance with His divine will, God created heaven and earth and all things in the universe.

Now how could they prove the validity of such a belief? To say that it is in the Bible merely begs the question. How do we know that the Bible story is historically accurate? How are we to interpret the biblical account, literally or metaphorically?

Akiba employs a well known proof, which is really a combination of two arguments, proof from the 'First Cause,' and the argument from 'Design.' Both were once extensively used, not only by Jewish thinkers but also by non-Jewish theologians. The argument from 'First Cause' submits that nothing in existence can be there by chance. There has to be a prime mover. Go back as far as you can. The bread is on the table because there was a baker who baked it. He obtained his flour because there was a farmer who grew the corn. The farmer produced his corn because the rains came down, the sun shone and the earth nurtured it. The rain, the sun and the earth are in existence because they were created within the scheme of the permanent laws of Nature. Those laws were established by a first power. That power is the creator—or God. Nothing exists by chance. There must always be a first cause. So Akiba can say that the clothes, the house, the furniture—all point to the fact that there was first of all a tailor, a builder and a carpenter. This is the argument of 'First Cause' which he held proves that the very existence of the world is sufficient proof of a prime Creator. The prophet Isaiah seems to employ the same argument of the 'First Cause' when he proclaims, *Lift up your eyes on high, and see: who hath created these?* (Isa. 40:26).

There is a further implication in our story which points to the proof by 'Design.' Briefly, this suggests that the nature of the universe is such that it could have been created only by a God of unlimited wisdom and power. The miraculous planetary system, the miracle of the human heart and brain, the petal of a flower and the myriad varieties in every species of life—all existing in accordance with an inexplicably intricate design—validate the belief in a divine wisdom and will which created it all. The psalmist made the same appeal to the argument from 'Design' when he sang, *The heavens declare the glory of God* (Ps. 19:2). Again, *When I behold thy heavens, the work of Thy fingers, the moon and the stars, which Thou hast established; What is man, that Thou art mindful of him . . . Yet Thou hast made him but little lower than the angels . . . Sheep and oxen, all of them . . . The fowl of the air, and fish of the sea . . . O Lord, our Lord, How glorious is Thy name in all the earth!* (Ibid. 8:4ff).

The arguments from 'First Cause' and 'Design' are not incontrovertible, but they served their purpose in an earlier age of theological discussion. For Judaism, what is incontrovertible is the belief that in the beginning there was God and that He is the source of all things in existence.

2

~

Creation Out of Nothing

A Gentile philosopher engaged Rabban Gamaliel in a discussion, in the course of which he said, "Your God is just a great artist who fashioned the world out of existing materials."

"And what were those materials?" Gamaliel asked him.

"Your Bible itself states them clearly enough in the opening verses of the Creation story where it says that the earth was *Tohu* (unformed) *and Bohu* (void), *and Darkness . . . , and the Wind* (spirit) *of God was on the Waters* (Gen. 1:2). So you see, before God created anything at all there was Tohu, Bohu, Darkness, Wind and Water. All these elements were in existence before creation, and God used them as His primary materials, out of which He began to create the universe."

Since the philosopher appealed to the Scriptures to make his point, Rabban Gamaliel then disproved each one by a similar appeal to the Bible to show that God created everything including Tohu and Bohu, the darkness, wind and the depths (*Ber. Rab.* 1:9).

*   *   *

This is typical of hundreds of similar anecdotes which tell of discussions held by the rabbis and their Gentile contemporaries. Sometimes the purpose of the Gentile disputant is to mock the rabbis and their Judaism. At other times, however, the motive of the discussion is honest enquiry where the Gentile genuinely wishes to learn the Jewish view on a particular matter. There is no reason to question the 'philosopher's' purpose in the present anecdote. His observation actually points to a serious problem in ancient theology which was, 'From what did God create the world?' Greek philosophy never could propound a theory of creation which held that God created the existing universe out of nothing. On the other hand, Jewish scholars were generally unwilling to limit God's omnipotence by submitting to any other theory, and in the main they rejected every other theory in favour of the doctrine of *creatio ex nihilo*—creation out of nothing. Even Maimonides, the greatest Jewish Aristotelian, who travels with Greek philosophy along many paths, leaves it on this issue.

In the main there were three theories of the origin of the world which were discussed by the philosophers. In his *Guide to the Perplexed* Maimonides lists them as follows. First, the theory that God brought the universe into existence out of a state of absolute nonexistence. At first, nothing existed except God. Then God brought forth, *ex nihilo*, all things by His will. "This is the first theory, and it is undoubtedly a fundamental principle of the Law of our teacher Moses; it is next in importance to the principle of God's unity" (*Guide*, 2:13). The second belief, and one which is known as the Platonic theory, is based on the principle that nothing can be formed from nothing, and it does not necessarily limit God's power by taking away from Him the ability to do the impossible, since "the nature of that which is impossible is constant . . . and there is no defect in the greatness of God when He is unable to produce a thing from nothing, because they consider this is one of the impossibilities" (Ibid.). The theory is then developed that prime matter existed all the time, by the side of God, and that so long as there was God there was also prime matter. One did not exist without the other. This does not mean that the prime matter is equal with God, for the relationship between the two is as the relationship of the clay to the potter, or the iron to the smith. The creator can fashion what he wills out of the substance which is there. The third theory of the origin of the world is that of Aristotle who claimed that since God is eternal and can never change His will to create the universe at a particular point in time, the process of creation is eternal, the motion of the spheres is eternal, and consequently the universe is uncreated. There is only natural development.

Maimonides makes no distinction, or little distinction, in his estimation of the second and third theories. To him they are both untenable, since even the second which posits the belief in an eternal prime matter would place something else which is eternal beside God. This initial enumeration by Maimonides of the three chief theories as we have listed them here is undoubtedly simplistic and avoids the various cross currents and later influences. Nevertheless, the above outline will serve our purpose to note the reaction of Jewish teachers.

The classical Jewish view on the subject provides a near unanimous belief in *creatio ex nihilo*. Among the talmudic rabbis, with their non-philosophical views, this is most certainly the case. Rabban Gamaliel's stand in his discussion with the Gentile enquirer is representative. He does not advance any argument on philosophical grounds. His view is derived from his reading of the Scriptures; and that is really sufficient proof for him. When we come to the masters of medieval Jewish philosophy, from Saadia in the tenth century and for at least the next five hundred years, we find the same insistence on the teaching—broached from a philosophical examination of the subject. Some, like Maimonides, thought of *creatio ex nihilo* as an essential doctrine of Judaism. Others held that while it should be embraced as a truth it is not necessary to regard it as a fundamental belief. What is fundamental in Judaism is the basic belief in God as the creator of the universe. We cannot postulate doctrinal teachings on how He created it.

3

~

One God

Abraham's family were all heathen idol-worshippers: his father was even an idol maker. One day Abraham was sent to the market with a basket full of idols made by his father, with instructions to sell them. But each time a customer came to buy, Abraham dissuaded him with a reasoned argument. "How old are you?" he asked one customer. "I am seventy years old" was the reply. "Then how ridiculous for you who have lived seventy years to worship an idol of wood which was made only yesterday!" Hearing this, the man threw the idol back into the basket and left. All day long Abraham confronted his customers with these and similar arguments, with the result that he made no sales.

Disappointed with Abraham's failure as a salesman, the family decided that he should stay at home and serve the idols as their priest. "What does the priest do?" asked Abraham. "He attends to all their needs" was the answer. In the middle of the afternoon a woman entered the house and brought a bowl of fine meal as an offering for the idols. "Here" she said, "give this to the gods." When she left, Abraham took a big stick and smashed all the idols to bits, leaving only the biggest idol untouched, and into its hands he fixed the stick. When his father returned home and saw all the havoc in his workshop, he asked Abraham what had happened. Whereupon his son replied, "During the afternoon someone brought in some food as a gift for the idols. As soon as she placed it down there was a scramble for the food, and this big one took the stick and began smashing up all the others so that he could have all the food for himself." His father became angry, "What nonsense are you telling me!" he shouted. "The idols are only pieces of wood or stone. They cannot see; they cannot hear; they cannot move or do anything. They do not live!" Abraham answered quietly, "Father, what you have said is true and I hope you realize the meaning of what you have just said."

Concluding that idol-worship and the pagan beliefs of his contemporaries were false, Abraham began to search for religious truth and his mind changed from one notion to another. At first he believed that the earth itself was God since it was benevolent and produced food for mankind. Then he pondered that the true God must be self-sufficient and does not need to be served by any other element, like the earth which needs the rain which enables it to grow the produce. So he began to think of the radiant sun as God since the sun is not serviced by anything else. But then the sun set and disappeared, its place taken by the moon and stars. Thinking on these phenomena Abraham concluded that neither the sun nor the moon represents the Deity since God is permanent. He does not change and is not replaced by anything else. He then affirmed, "There must be a separate Power Who made the earth, the sun and the moon and all existence." In this way Abraham gradually came to the belief in the only One God, Creator of all things (*Mid. Hag.* on Genesis; *Ber. Rab.* 38:13).

*   *   *

Abraham is the first patriarch of the Hebrew people. In the tradition he earns this status because he was the first one to recognize God as a single Supreme Being, the sole Creator of the universe and all things in it. Abraham lived in a pagan civilization where the worship of idols was normal. In his religious beliefs Abraham was the exception, and this uniqueness gives him the rank of the pioneer of the monotheistic faith of Judaism.

The theology of Judaism is grounded in its history, and the beginnings of that history are discovered in the story of Abraham the iconoclast who was the first to recognize the truth about the only One God. While the Bible states that God chose Abraham it says nothing at all about the patriarch before he received the call of God, when he was over seventy years old, to leave his country, his kindred and his and his father's house (Gen. 12:1). But the above midrashim fill the gaps by telling that it was Abraham who chose God. And in a very real sense that has been the role and even the purpose of the Jews in history—to be witnesses to the truth of the only One God. The rabbis have a perceptive saying that the deeds of the patriarchs were an indication pointing to the subsequent deeds of their descendants. Monotheism was the central doctrine of Judaism from earliest times and has remained so throughout Jewish history. *Hear, O Israel: the Lord is our God, the Lord is One* (Deut. 6:4) is the basic theological doctrine of Judaism. It has often been said, though with some opposition, that Judaism has no dogma, a fundamental tenet without which the faith could not exist. However, even the proponents of a "dogma-less" Judaism affirm that belief in the unity of God is seen as a dogma. Without that tenet, the structure of Jewish beliefs falls to the ground. It is significant that the story of Jewish heroism and sacrifice records the martyrdom of countless Jews who willingly suffered death rather than show disloyalty to their faith in the only One God. Throughout its history the Jews remained protestors against pagan idolatry, Persian dualism and Christian trinitarianism. The faithful Jew would tolerate no compromise with the doctrine of God's unity.

But this central teaching is not of theological significance only. It also has vital sociological importance. Since there is only One God who created all mankind then all men and women are, in relationship to each other, as brothers and sisters—all created by the one God. The prophet Malachi taught this truth in his memorable words, *Have we not all one father, hath not one God created us all?* (Mal. 2:10). The doctrine of One God also supports the teachings about a single universe with a cosmic law which unifies all existence: for Nature is also one, deriving from a single central principle of creation. Further, it means that the One God who is the source of the inspiration which came to the law-givers and leaders of men wants the law and the ideals of justice to be the same for all men.

4

~

What is Man?

When God was about to create man He was surrounded by several groups of angels who offered different opinions. Some were for creating him; others were against. And each group had its reasons for urging as it did. The angel Lovingkindness was in favor of man being created, and he said, "Man will perform many acts of lovingkindness." But the angel Truth argued against his being created saying, "Man will be full of lies." The angel Righteousness was in favor because he believed that a man would be capable of doing acts of righteousness. But against this was the angel Peace who said, "He will be full of strife." Faced with such conflicting counsel, what did God do? He took Truth and threw it down so that it broke into many pieces, leaving the majority opinion in favor of man; and He then proceeded with His plan to create man.

But the creation of Adam was not so simple and even God had to consider several problems. God had made the universe by mixing the heavenly and earthly materials in equal proportions so that there would be a true harmony between the different elements. Thus the first day's creation is hailed with the words, *In the beginning God created the heavens and the earth* (Gen. 1:1)—a combination of the heavenly and the earthly. On the second day God said, *Let there be a firmament* (Ibid. v. 6)—heavenly. On the third day God said, *Let the earth bring forth* (Ibid. v. 11)—earthly. On the fourth day He said, *Let there be lights* (Ibid. v. 14)—heavenly. On the fifth day He said, *Let the waters swarm* (Ibid. v. 20)—earthly. So God maintained an equal measure of the heavenly and the earthly in the creation of the universe. Then when God was about to create Adam on the sixth day He said, "If I create him from heavenly material then those elements will prevail over the material. But if I create him from earthly matter then the earthly elements will have numerical superiority over the heavenly ones." What did He do? He created Adam from a mixture of the two and he was thus made from an equal measure of both. And so the Bible records, *And God created man out of the dust of the earth* (material) *and He breathed into his nostrils the spirit of life* (heavenly) (*Ber. Rab.* 8:8; 12:8).

*   *   *

These two pieces of folklore have been brought together because they belong to a single theme—the nature of man. God is described as consulting with the angels prior to His creation of Adam. Why? There was no consultation before the creation of anything else! It is because there is an element of doubt and hesitation in the divine plan on the whole question of the nature of man. The angels are divided in their opinions and in their counsel. All this of course means that man himself is full of contradictions. Is he essentially good or basically evil? Is he a spark of the Divine, or is he no more than dust and ashes? The psalmist echoes some of this doubt when he cries out in wonderment, *What is man that Thou art mindful of him?* (Ps. 8:5). It is not only the character of man which is problematic. His lowly nature leads to his lowly destiny. What is the superiority of man over beast? *For that which befalleth the sons of men befalleth beasts; even one thing befalleth them; as one dieth so dieth the other; yea they have all one breath; so that man hath no preeminence above a beast; for all is vanity* (Ecc. 3:19). There is evidence enough of man's lowly character and his evil propensities. The history of the human race is the sad record of man's greed, hatred and murder.

But that is only one part of the picture. It is true that the Bible and rabbinic literature contain reference to the baser aspects of human nature. And it is true that man has a tendency to lie, to make war and voraciously to pursue the material and the sensual. Yet it is just as true that he is capable of pursuing deeds of lovingkindness and justice, and to aspire to holy and spiritual things in life. So God accepted the counsel of the angels Lovingkindness and Righteousness. He also planted within man a spark of His divine spirit by breathing into him the soul of life. If man does have a tendency to do evil, it is more significant that he has the capacity to do good. That is the uniqueness of man; that precisely because he is made up of elements of the ignoble and the noble, that he can experience the challenge to reach for the sublime.

It has been suggested by most historians that, on balance, the human record shows more evidence of progress in ethical values. This progress is marked by advances in education and even in man's capacity to live and to care. How else could he have been moved to build schools and hospitals? How else could history be filled with heroes of the spirit, with saintly men and women whose self-sacrificing lives were dedicated in love to the welfare of their fellow men? It is of course sadly true that the satanic horrors perpetrated by Nazi Germany in that country's Hitlerian period suggests that even in modern times a sophisticated and highly educated society can sink to the lowest levels of barbarism. Yet it is just as significant that the civilized world took notice of that reversion to bestial savagery, went to war and uprooted the evil. That there are remnants of murderous primitivism still extant in the world of today does not affect the argument that the overall forces of good are more widespread.

It is relevant to our theme that in Judaism there is little or no concept of the notion of "original sin" which holds that man's destiny is to sin unless he is saved by the grace of God (which in Christianity is introduced by a religious sacrament). Our stories imply that man has a tendency to sin. But that is very different from the concept that he has the destiny to sin. Furthermore, the important optimistic approach of Judaism puts forth the teaching that the human tendency to sin can be overcome by the innate spiritual power with which man is endowed. Maimonides taught that the creation of man was the crown of all God's creative activity: and the psalmist celebrates the Jewish teaching about the nature of man when he sings . . . *Thou hast made him but little lower than the angels, and hast crowned him with glory and honour* (Ps. 8:6).

TORAH

5

~

The Crowns of the Torah

When Moses was on Mount Sinai to receive the Torah, he saw God adding crowns on several letters each time they appeared in the Torah. "What is the purpose of these little crowns? Couldn't the Torah be given without them?" he asked.

And God answered, "Some time in the future there will be a great teacher by the name of Akiba ben Yosef who will expound numerous laws which he will deduce from every one of these little lines."

Moses was intrigued and expressed the wish to see this man Akiba. God agreed to the request and gave Moses the power to glance into the future. "Turn around" God said. Moses did so and found himself in the academy of Rabbi Akiba, fifteen hundred years later.

He sat at the back of the lecture hall as Akiba interpreted the law before rows of disciples. But what he heard was all very strange to him. He didn't understand what Akiba was teaching, as it all seemed very different from his own law.

Moses became sad, because he thought that his law would be forgotten and replaced by something new. Then suddenly he heard one of the students question Akiba, "Master, what is the source and authority for this law which you have been teaching us?"

Akiba gave his firm and immediate answer, "The source and authority is that it derives from the Torah of Moses our teacher, which he received on Mount Sinai." When Moses heard Akiba's reply, he was content, and he went back to his own world (*Men.* 29b).

*   *   *

There is a little more added to the story as told in the Talmud, but that need not concern us just now, because the folklore just given is complete in itself and has some basic things to teach us about the nature of Torah. We will touch on only two of those concepts.

The first is that the Torah laws are not changeless, but develop throughout the ages. If this were not so, then the whole of Jewish law would have been contained in the Bible. In fact Judaism would have stopped with the Bible as its only source, and there would have been no place for the Talmud and the vast rabbinic literature which developed in later ages.

But the truth is that there are biblical laws which were suspended or even abolished by authoritative rabbis (e.g., trial by ordeal, Num. 5:29–31); some laws were changed from their literal meaning (e.g., *lex talionis*, Ex. 21:24–26, Lev. 24:19–20); while other laws were adapted in a way as to make them work in a new age (e.g., Hillel's prosbul).

And that is not all. There are many laws and customs in Judaism which are not in the Bible at all (e.g., the post-biblical festival of Hanukkah). Further, there are numerous laws in Jewish religious life which could never have been understood or accepted without the contemporary interpretations, amendments and additions of the rabbis. How would we know the many details even of such basic institutions as the Sabbath, the festival observances, kashrut and daily prayer, the particulars of which are not in the Bible at all?

This leads us to a very important conclusion, which is that our Judaism does not rest on the Bible alone, but on the Bible as it has been interpreted throughout the ages. This is the Judaism of history, the Judaism of the rabbis, the Judaism of tradition with ordered growth, the Judaism of authentic interpretation and adaptation. It is the Judaism taught by Akiba in our story.

The interesting thing is that Moses didn't recognize his own Torah, because he could not envisage how it would be interpreted and adapted from age to age, fifteen hundred years into the distant future. This is our first lesson, that the rabbis used their powers of exposition, and through their interpretations there was change to meet the new conditions of the age.

The second lesson touches upon the important question of authority. Who gives the rabbis, or anyone else, the authority to interpret a written law in the Bible, let alone to amend or suspend it, or to add a religious practice which is not in the Bible at all? In our story, Akiba connects his teaching with the sinaitic tradition. Some scholars take this literally, so that, according to them all the interpretations were given by God to Moses on Sinai, and the entire oral law is sinaitic just as the written law is from Sinai. Therefore when an accepted scholar teaches a new law and argues that it is sinaitic, he does not need any greater authority. In fact the entire problem of authority is brushed aside once it is held that the oral interpretation is also from Sinai. Everything that is taught in later ages is traced back to the Torah of Moses. In this spirit a rabbinic saying has it that at any time, whatever an authentic and recognized Jewish teacher expounds owes its origin to the law of Moses at Sinai.

On the other hand, there are scholars who stress the thought that from age to age the Torah has to be freshly and independently interpreted. After all, what Akiba was teaching was new to his disciples. It was not understood even by Moses himself, because the Judaism of Akiba was not and could not be identical with the Judaism of Moses, since it had to be explicated and interpreted for a different age.

And this has been a characteristic, and even a challenge, in the history of Judaism. The authority for that kind of rabbinic function is actually found in the Bible itself, where the people are exhorted to obey the teachings of their contemporary judges and religious leaders (Deut. 17:19ff).

The rabbis accepted this serious responsibility, but traditionally they tried to connect their teachings to the Bible, wherever that was possible, so that they could create a formal link between the Torah of Moses and their own nuances. They thus established the principle of an organic unity between the written law of Moses and the oral law of history.

6

~

The Torah Belongs to Man

One day the sages in the high rabbinic assembly were debating whether an oven made in a certain shape and known as the oven of *akhnai* was subject to defilement or not. All the rabbis agreed that, like any other earthenware object, it could be exposed to ritual defilement. But there was one exception. Rabbi Eliezer ben Hyrcanus declared that it could not be defiled.

Now by the accepted rules of the academy, the majority opinion prevailed. Under those circumstances all that would have happened was that Rabbi Eliezer's view would have gone into the talmudic record and that would have been the end of the debate. But Eliezer was a stern antagonist and absolutely unyielding in his opinion. As far as he was concerned, he was right and all the others were wrong. Being unable to convince his colleagues by argument he resorted to the most bizarre and dramatic methods in his attempts to prove his point.

"Let the carob tree which grows outside prove that I am right" he said. And the carob tree outside the academy uprooted itself from its place and moved away to a distance of one hundred cubits.

"We cannot accept such a sign as an argument in our debate" said the rabbis.

"If I am right, then let the waters of the stream which flow past the academy confirm it." said Eliezer.

The rabbis looked outside and saw that the stream of water had begun to flow in the opposite direction. But they remained unimpressed and said, "This cannot be accepted as a proof in an halakhic dispute.

Eliezer was not to be repulsed. "In that case let the walls of this academy prove that I am right!" he retorted. Immediately the walls began to incline inwards threatening to collapse altogether. Whereupon Rabbi Joshua, one of the leading rabbis of the assembly, rebuked them. "What has this dispute got to do with you?" he angrily asked. "Leave us to look after our own affairs!" So the walls remained slanted. They did not fall, out of deference to Rabbi Joshua; but neither did they return to their upright position, out of respect for Rabbi Eliezer.

Not to be put off, Rabbi Eliezer tried once more. This time he appealed to the highest authority. "If you are not convinced by what has happened so far" he pleaded, "then let a *bat kol*, a heavenly voice, support me!" Thereupon the assembled sages heard a heavenly voice declare, "Leave off your disputation with Eliezer, for his decision is the correct one."

There was momentary consternation in the academy. But Rabbi Joshua soon stood up and reproached the *bat kol* for interfering in the rabbinic debate. "The Torah is no longer in heaven. It has already been given to us and it contains the instruction that we follow the majority opinion. Therefore we take no notice even of a heavenly voice."

A daring but significant epilogue has it that some time later one of the rabbis met with Elijah the prophet and asked him about God's reaction to the incident. Elijah told him that God gladly accepted the rabbinic stand and acknowledged, "My children have prevailed over Me! My children have prevailed over Me! (*Bab. Metz.* 59b).

*   *   *

This is one of the most famous of all disputations in the Talmud. The actual debate was simply about the possibility of the ritual defilement of an oven called *tannur akhnai*, literally "a snake-like oven," because of its circular shape. The technical and ritualistic details do not concern us now. All that it is necessary to state here is that in a religious culture which connects physical and spiritual purity into a single system, the debate was one of some importance. But it is also significant for another reason which is our present topic.

The rabbis of the academy all ruled that the *akhnai* oven, like any other earthenware appliance, was subject to defilement if it came into contact with any substance which transmits impurity. But there was one rabbi who disagreed with this view, Rabbi Eliezer ben Hyrcanus, and he held that the *akhnai* oven could not be defiled. Now in accordance with the procedure in the ancient schools, the majority view was decisive. This was an aspect of the healthy democratic system in rabbinic Judaism, and it was especially important at that time when Jewish law and teaching was being minutely examined, clarified and codified. The Talmud reflects the process of healthy debate and gives us a picture of free, open and intellectual controversy. But ultimately the law had to be finalized and a single opinion could not serve as a veto on the majority opinion. Without respect for the disciplined acceptance of the majority view there would have been total chaos, with every teacher competing with the others to establish his own law.

There is another point which needs to be emphasized. How could the rabbis refuse to obey the *bat kol* or heavenly voice, which was like a divine oracle, and which proclaimed that Eliezer's view was the right one? After all, God gave the Law, and God's will is an expression of the final authority. It is therefore worth pointing out here that the rabbinic attitude illustrated in the rejection of the *bat kol* is startlingly revolutionary. In essence the rabbis affirmed that once the Torah had been given to them, it was their responsibility to face it with all its manifold challenges, and to grapple with it, day and night, in order to make it a practical guide for daily living in their own world. No angel, supernatural event or even heavenly voice could be allowed to interfere or detract from their responsibility or diminish their authority. The Torah is meant to be lived in this world, not in another. The Law belongs to man, and the rabbis are its sole adjudicators.

So the story has tremendously important implications. By insisting on the democratic character of rabbinic legislation where the majority view has to be followed, they encouraged a halakhic process which ultimately expressed the opinions and feelings of the community as a whole led by their rabbinic teachers. But even more important is the fact that the story points to an address for the authority which interprets the Law. That address is the rabbis. By implication it means that they alone are responsible for making the Law serve as a practical guide in all its manifestations and changes. For this reason, the rabbis of the academy insisted on retaining their authority and resisted the injection of supernatural signs or even the oracle of the *bat kol*. As far as they were concerned, the Torah, having been given to them from Sinai, was now their responsibility to interpret and to legislate. That responsibility was theirs alone. The little epilogue suggests that even God "agreed."

7

For Love of Torah

As a young student in the school of Shemaiah and Avtalyon, Hillel had to follow a menial job in order to support himself. He became a wood cutter, and half of what he earned each day went to support himself and his family: the remainder he paid to the caretaker at the school house in order to gain admission to the lectures.

One day—it happened to be a Friday morning in the winter—Hillel was altogether without money, and the unsympathetic door keeper at the school house refused to let him in. Undaunted by the heartless rebuff, Hillel went to the back of the school, climbed to the roof, put his ear to the open skylight and was able to listen to the lessons given in the room below by his illustrious teachers. When the lessons were finished, everyone went home to prepare for the Sabbath, but Hillel was fatigued and fell asleep. During the night there was a snow-fall and the poor sleeping Hillel remained under a layer of snow.

Next morning the two teachers entered the study house and found it extraordinarily dark. "This is strange" said one of them. "Let's see what has happened." On going outside they saw the inert frozen figure of a young man and when they brought him down from the roof they recognized Hillel. Carrying him into the study room they immediately lit a fire, heated some oil and revived his frozen body. "It is a religious duty to break the Sabbath to save a life" they said. "But for such a one as Hillel we can also be sure that he will bring many thousands to the joy of Sabbath observance."

The prophecy of the two teachers was realized in the subsequent career of Hillel who adopted as a motto in life, "Always try to bring people close to the Torah" (*Yoma* 35b).

*   *   *

Hillel lived in the first century during the last decades of the Second Temple. He was born in Babylon but went to Jerusalem to study under the distinguished teachers Shemaiah and Avtalyon. Many stories have been told about his wisdom and humility, his patience and his love for his fellow man. But the most important thing about Hillel was his central place in the development of rabbinic law at a time when it was particularly critical for the written system of biblical rules to encompass oral interpretation, extensions and modifications which could make the law into a dynamic system governing all aspects of daily life with its varied nuances to meet the changing conditions in the social and economic life of the community. In this work, Hillel stands in the forefront as the builder of classical rabbinic Judaism.

Because of his preeminence in the history of rabbinic leadership Hillel is often referred to as Hillel the Great or Hillel the Elder. He was appointed the *nasi*, or head of the Sanhedrin, which was the highest and the authoritative assembly of rabbinic scholars.

The above story is one of the most famous legends which have accumulated around his name, and it is included here as an illustration of a basic value of Jewish life.

We shall deal in a moment with the real lesson of the story. But before getting to it we might briefly note the strange situation where payment had to be made to the school doorman in order to gain entry into the school! One does not come across such a practice elsewhere in the literature. Also there was no such thing as tuition fees for the teachers. In fact rabbinic ethic more or less rules out payment of any kind, and the teachers of the academy earned their living by following other occupations. Thus Shammai was a builder, Rabbi Joshua was a blacksmith and others were farmers. It is of course probable that in our story, the money given to the caretaker was an emolument which the man received from the students for looking after the place. We don't know. However, the situation is hard to understand when we read that the man received from Hillel as much money as the poor student would spend to keep himself and his family! It is also not clear if the teachers were even aware of the entrance by payment system. And if they had been aware of it, would they have put a stop to it?

The full version of the story concludes with the information that from that time onwards Hillel, at least, was able to enter the study house without further payment to the doorman.

Now for the main teaching. There are several great loves in Jewish life. There is love of God, love of fellow man, love of the people of Israel and love of the land of Israel. All of them occupy a central place in the literature of Judaism. In line together with these great theological and ethical values is the love of Torah.

Torah is a value which is not always fully understood because it is not easy to explain. The term can be understood in any one of several ways. In its most limited meaning it refers to the Scroll of the Law or the Five Books of Moses—the Pentateuch. These books contain the first part of the biblical record, the Creation stories, the stories of the patriarchs and the Hebrew tribe, the enslavement in Egypt and the Exodus, the revelation at Sinai, the declaration of the Ten Commandments and the promulgation of all the other laws given to the children of Israel in the wilderness on their way to independence in the land of Israel. The Five Books of Moses are of first importance since they include the religious constitution of the people of Israel together with its basic laws and Israel's covenant with God.

In a slightly wider sense the term Torah can refer to all the books of the Bible; not only the first five, but all twenty four books, from Genesis to Chronicles. As a unified collection they are known by the Hebrew acrostic *Tanakh*, a word made up of three Hebrew letters which are abbreviations of the three sections of the full Bible—Torah, *Neviim* and *Ketuvim*, viz., the Pentateuch, the Prophets and the later Writings. All of that collection is Torah. But strictly speaking it is only the written Torah, i.e., all that which was written down and included in the written canon of the Scriptures.

But that is not all there is to Torah. If the written Bible was the totality of Torah, then Jewish thought and teaching, especially its legal norms, could have become ossified and in time largely irrelevant to all the changing conditions of society.

So at this point we come to the crucial concept of the oral Torah. This is the vast corpus of interpretation, exposition, debate and decision which were undertaken throughout many generations in a detailed effort to explore every part of the written law. This was an ongoing process which must have begun at the earliest times of Jewish legal activity and went on in every subsequent age. The high peak of rabbinic interpretation was the talmudic period which stretched well over five centuries culminating in the redaction of the Babylonian Talmud in 500 C.E. Everything that was taught following the canonization of the written Bible is the oral law, and it is all an integral part of Torah. When the Jew speaks of Torah, mostly he means much more than the written Bible: he includes at least also the oral law of the rabbis as redacted in the Talmud. He recognizes that the oral law is part of the main body of the Torah. It is like the extended arm of the written law so it is part of the body of Torah. On its own, the written law could not have survived and could not have become the final constitution of Judaism. This can soon be seen and understood by a consideration of the following. There are laws in the Bible which the rabbis actually read out of Jewish life because they no longer had any relevance. At the same time there are many laws which are not in the Bible at all but were promulgated by the rabbis long after the close of the Bible period, in the light of new historical events and circumstances. In addition there are numerous laws in the Bible which could not and in fact were not accepted without detailed explanation and interpretation—all of which has its place in the oral law and ultimately written down in the Talmud and in later works. So we are led to a most important conclusion which has to be kept in mind by every student of Judaism. We have made this point in another context, but it bears repetition here. That is, Judaism does not rest on the Bible alone, but on the Bible as it has been interpreted and developed in the course of history and tradition. And the Bible together with the whole of that interpretation which we call the oral law is Torah.

But Torah does not stop even there. In a significant way Torah grows all the time, and it continues to grow even in our day as well. This is because in every Jewish community throughout the world Jewish scholars have explored the sources to discover new meaning in Torah. They have written commentaries, glosses and codes on Jewish life so that in the widest sense Torah will include every search for its meaning right up to our time.

Now it has to be noted, however briefly, that the written law could be interpreted and adapted by the oral law only in accordance with certain hermeneutic principles. In other words the legal process from the written law to its oral extension was an organic growth, worked out in accordance with logical rules of expounding a text. The first set of such principles was laid down by Hillel, and that makes his role in rabbinic Judaism especially important. The need to create the enabling rules for the Torah's growth must have inspired Hillel right from the beginning of his career as a Torah scholar, and our story illustrates his extreme passion for Torah study, even to the extent of self-sacrifice, since he valued Torah more than his daily bread. In fact the talmudic source of our story prefaces the tale by saying that if anyone should ever make poverty an excuse for not studying Torah, let him remember the story of the poor student Hillel, and learn from it.

There are of course numerous other tales which illustrate the same theme, but our popular story of Hillel still stands out as an example of the Jew's total dedication to Torah and its study. That created the civilization of Judaism, and made for the survival not only of Judaism but of the Jewish people.

8

~

The Greater Love

For the first forty years of his life, the famous Rabbi Akiba was totally ignorant, and was even illiterate. He was a very mature man before he began to study. It all happened like this.

Akiba worked for some years as a shepherd for one of the wealthiest men in Jerusalem, a strange man whom people nicknamed Kalba Savua. This man had a daughter, Rachel, who fell in love with the hard working and good shepherd. She recognized Akiba's sterling character and knew that the only thing which he lacked was a formal education. On her initiative they became secretly betrothed on condition that Akiba leave the fields and go to study. Akiba agreed to the condition and he made his way to the academy of Rabbis Eliezer and Joshua in Lydda. There he started as a complete beginner, but his prodigious labors enabled him to advance. He remained with the great teachers for twelve years and became not only an outstanding scholar but also a famous teacher with a massive following of disciples.

Meanwhile things were not good on the domestic front. In fact they had been very bad for Rachel for some time. When her father learned of her secret betrothal to the ignorant shepherd, he expelled her from his house, and vowed that she would never have any benefit from his wealth. So Rachel lived in dire poverty and was even taunted by her neighbors who scoffed at her for her "living widowhood." But she was firm in her resolve to leave Akiba to concentrate on his studies. She was sure that the day would come when he would return.

That day came. An old man told Rachel that Akiba was back, accompanied by several thousands of students. When she heard that, Rachel said, "I don't care if he remains in the academy for another twelve years. I know that he will still come back to me and be even more famous than he is now." When Akiba learned of his wife's remark he said, "She really means that. Her own devotion to Torah study for me is the strongest thing in her life." So he returned with his disciples to his own academy in Bnai Brak and pursued his teaching there for several more years. Finally, when he returned to Rachel he was accompanied by no less than twenty-four thousand students who were dedicated to him as the greatest teacher of their time.

When Rachel saw him at the head of the huge procession, she fell to the ground and began to kiss his feet. The attendants of the great rabbi were horrified, since they did not know who this strange dishevelled woman was. They rushed forward to push her away, but Akiba stopped them. "Leave her" he said. "Whatever I know and whatever you know we owe only to her."

Although many years had passed, the wealthy Kalba Savua was still alive. But he was now a troubled and lonely old man, obsessed with one idea before it was too late. He now wanted to annul his vow by which, years before, he had cut off his daughter from all his estate and possessions. He had no idea what had happened to her and her shepherd husband Akiba. Hearing that a great scholar and authority on the law had arrived, he went to see him to request the rabbi to arrange the technical and legal procedures to have his vow annulled. Of course he did not recognize Akiba, and as he told his story he believed he was talking to a total stranger.

Akiba asked him, "Would you have disowned them had the man been a scholar?"

"Rabbi" he answered, "the man was a complete ignoramus. He couldn't even read! Why, if he had known only the smallest thing about the Torah I would not have rejected them."

"I want you to know that I am that man" Akiba said simply.

Of course after that there was a warm and happy reconciliation. Kalba Savua's vow was formally annulled and he gave Rachel and Akiba half of his estate (*Ket.* 62b–63a).

*   *   *

That story may not strike the reader as being very romantic if we are concerned only with the emotions of the love of a man and a woman.

How could they be parted for twelve years? Then when Akiba does return, how could Rachel suggest that he might go away again for another twelve years? And Akiba agrees! Of course we are dealing with elements of legend and we are therefore entitled to assume that there is a great deal of exaggeration. If it makes us feel any better then we can take that part of the story with a big pinch of salt. It doesn't really matter for our purpose, which is to investigate the moral of the story as it was told and widely accepted. What is the motive of the story teller? It is his lesson which remains the central thesis of the talmudic legend.

In this as well as in other stories we see that the great passion in Akiba's life was Torah study. It had to be spread among the people, and there was no higher value than that, since it was the only thing which could ensure the survival of the Jewish people. By the time of Akiba the Jews had lost their independence, their land, their Temple, their priests and their kings. All the former elements of national life had been destroyed. So other ways had to be employed to secure the continuity of the Jewish people. The covenant of Israel with God and the divine promise of God's redemption had to be kept alive. The transformation was from a physical nationalism to a spiritual peoplehood. Without national independence the Jews still had to be able to breathe the spirit of freedom; without a land of their own they still had to live within clearly recognized spiritual boundaries; without a Temple every Jewish home was to become a sanctuary in miniature pervaded by an ambiance of sanctity. Without a king or an army the Jewish people were to become strengthened by God's spirit and to acknowledge Him as the Supreme King of Kings. In a period of history when the Roman emperor was venerated as a god whose statues were mounted in all parts of the country the spiritual resistance of the Jews was of course dangerously revolutionary, but it was revolutionary also in the sense that it created a new kind of Jewish people. How was this transformation effected? It needed the teaching of radical new directions in Jewish life. And that could be done only by developing and strengthening a daily discipline for the Jew which was rooted in Torah teaching, and making it the heritage of every Jew. There was nothing quite as important. The rabbis of that age knew what was at stake. It was a question of the survival or death of the Jewish religion, and therefore of the Jewish people. No other period in Jewish history had to confront such a challenge; at least not to the same extent. This process of national transformation to equip the people to live as a spiritual entity instead of as a nationally independent group did not start with Rabbi Akiba. The great hero of the period of change was really Rabban Johanan ben Zakkai who lived about sixty years before Akiba.

But obviously such a national transformation took time and was led by many great teachers and leaders. Rabbi Akiba was one of the foremost master builders of the new people and his story illustrates the extent of the centrality which they placed on the study and dissemination of Torah. In the result, the Jewish people survived because of the life and work of leaders like Akiba, who made the Torah their first priority.

Before we leave our story, it is proper to point out that Akiba is not the only hero in the legend. In fact, Rachel is even the greater hero. He at least had his work cut out in the challenging discipline of the academy. But she was left languishing in poverty for many years, the victim also of unkindly jibes. Furthermore, it was Rachel who took the initiative—unusual in Jewish life in those days. She recognized the ethical qualities in Akiba. She fell in love with him. She knew that all he lacked was a formal education. And it was she who suggested their betrothal on the condition that he go away to study. For that value she sacrificed her youth and many years of marriage and companionship. Akiba's remark to his disciples correctly sums up the proper evaluation of Rachel's magnificent role in the epic story, "Whatever I know, and whatever you know, we owe only to her!" As if to emphasize Rachel's decisive part in Akiba's advancement, additional rabbinic stories report that Akiba gave his wife the most costly and beautiful jewelry as a token of his great love and appreciation of her sacrifice. Among those precious items was a fabulous golden headpiece, known as a "golden Jerusalem," which was a symbol of Rachel's brilliant example of devotion to Torah scholarship.

9

Stronger than Death

When the Roman rulers of Palestine issued their order that teaching Torah would be a capital offence there was a danger that the study of Torah would cease and in time it might be forgotten with serious danger to the future of Judaism. So Rabbi Akiba went on gathering together as many disciples as he could and continued to teach.

One day he met an acquaintance named Pappus. This man was not so dedicated to Torah and had spent many of his years outside the Holy Land acquiring some Greek culture. But he remained a friend of Akiba and on his return to the Holy Land the friendship was renewed. One day he saw Akiba expounding the Law before a gathering of his disciples and when the lesson was over he tried to dissuade his friend from risking his life.

"Don't you know" he said "that if the Romans hear what you are doing they will execute you? Does all this warrant losing your life? Why don't you lay low until the danger is over and then you can take up your teaching again!"

"O Pappus, Pappus" said Akiba. "I thought that you were a wise man: but your comment is not worthy of you! Let me tell you a story." And the sage continued with the following parable.

One day the cunning fox was out walking close to the river. On looking into the water he saw shoals of fish frantically swimming away in all directions. "What is all the hurry?" he asked the fish. And they answered him, "Every day, just about this time a fisherman comes with his nets which he throws into the water and catches many of our brothers. So we have to hide from him and swim away as far as we can from the place where he throws his nets."

On hearing this, the wily fox said to the fish, "You needn't worry yourselves any more or feel any fear for your lives. Come with me into my cave in the woods. I have lived there for many years and I have never seen a single fisherman enter my cave. Come with me and you will be safe." The fish laughed at the fox because they immediately saw through his plan. "Foolish fox" they said. "Why do people think you are crafty. You are really very foolish. If we are not safe in the water which is our element and where we can breathe naturally, how much more dangerous would it be if we left the water and went to live where we cannot exist at all."

The meaning of the parable was clear. If the Jews were in danger even when they were living in their own element which is the Torah, how much less secure would they be if they forsook it.

Some time later Akiba was arrested by the Romans and was put in jail to await his execution. Who should he see as a fellow prisoner but his friend Pappus! "What offence brings you here?" asked Akiba. And Pappus answered him, "Blessed are you Akiba. You were arrested for teaching Torah—which is our element enabling us to live. As for me, the Romans threw me into jail on some trumped up charge. You will die a martyr sanctifying the Name of God, the Torah and the Jewish people. I will perish in a meaningless death" (*Ber.* 61b).

*   *   *

The Hadrianic persecution of the Jews in the second century brought the most severe suffering which the oppressed Jewish people ever had to bear under Roman rule. The economic misery brought on by heavy taxation, the exile and the poverty, the torture and the imprisonments were made all the more unbearable by the oppressive Roman laws against the practice of Judaism. Among the Roman ordinances were several which prohibited the teaching of Torah and the ordination of new rabbis. By those measures the Romans believed that they could destroy Judaism once and for all. But rabbinic scholars were ordained and the teaching of Torah and the development of the law continued in spite of the obvious danger of being caught and executed. Rabbi Akiba was one of several outstanding rabbis who continued to disseminate Torah knowledge among the people, and he suffered martyrdom as a result. While the above story is told about Rabbi Akiba, it can symbolize the sacrifice of many of his colleagues.

The lesson of the story is really obvious and does not call for much explanation. In any case we have already emphasized part of the teaching in two earlier stories. But first, it is perhaps useful to point out that the martyrdom of Akiba is accepted as historical. That he was executed for ignoring the Roman prohibition against teaching Torah also matches everything we know about the Roman oppression of the Jews during the Hadrianic period. The Talmud even records the tradition that Akiba died after the most cruel tortures were inflicted upon him and as he proclaimed the declaration of the Shema. "All these years I have considered the meaning of the words, *And thou shalt love the Lord thy God, with all thy heart, and with all thy soul and with all thy might* (Deut. 6:5). To love God with all one's heart means with total sincerity of faith and feeling. To love Him with all one's might means, as our sages have explained, with all one's worldly possessions. But to love Him with all one's soul means to love God even with one's life itself. Now that I have the chance to carry out this ultimate commandment, shall I question it or hesitate for a single moment?" And Akiba expired even as he proclaimed . . . *Adonai Ehad*, "The Lord is One."

But obviously, the main teaching of the story of Akiba's martyrdom is once again the theology of the centrality of Torah in Jewish life. The rabbis clearly understood that, especially in the historical circumstances of their difficult time, Judaism would be lost and the Jews would therefore fade out of history if they could not be held together by the Torah and its laws. Without a land of their own and without the Temple as a central national and unifying shrine it was only the study of Torah and dedication to its teachings which could serve as the unifying bond, creating a religious culture which could take the place of the lost land and Temple. Without the Torah, there would be no hope for any kind of Jewish future. Hence the supremacy of Torah in rabbinic theology also had a national importance which at times could call for the ultimate sacrifice of martyrdom.

10

The Bible is True

When Joseph was a slave in Potiphar's household, he was extremely successful in everything he undertook. Potiphar recognized the extra-ordinary ability of his Hebrew slave so he put him in charge of his entire household and estate.

Now Joseph's success went to his head and he began to have a great time, eating and drinking in his master's house, and dressing his hair in the most modern Egyptian styles of the day. He was very pleased with himself. God then said, "Your father mourns for you in sackcloth and ashes, while you are feasting and adorning yourself! By your life, I will set the she-bear on you!" The 'she-bear' was Potiphar's wife who had her own personal designs for Joseph.

Joseph was less than twenty years old at the time, and he was filled with the lusty hot blood of youth. Potiphar's wife was infatuated with the handsome youth and tried to seduce him. Every day she tried all sorts of feminine charms, but Joseph's sense of responsibility to his master remained firm, and her attempts to seduce him failed. She even became ill because of her unrequited love, and when her lady friends asked her why she was looking so pale she decided to put them also to the test by exposing them to Joseph's youthful handsomeness.

So one day she invited a group of them to her home, and after they had made themselves comfortable in her salon, she provided each of them with a fruit and a knife to cut it. Then as they were cutting their fruit she called in Joseph on some pretext. The ladies all stared at him. They were bewitched by his looks, and couldn't take their eyes

off him, as they continued to peel and cut their fruit. In the process
they cut their hands. Then after Joseph left the room, Mrs. Potiphar
said to them, "See what happened to you all after looking at Joseph
for just a few minutes. Now you can understand my condition when I
see him every day!"

Our legend has an interesting sequel in the Midrash. A Roman
lady once said to Rabbi Jose, "I don't believe that Joseph rejected all
the advances of Potiphar's wife. Here is a lusty young man with all the
opportunity in the world. His master is away all day, and the wife is
more than willing! Can you tell me that Joseph would not give in to
her? Your Bible is covering up for him and not telling the truth!"

Rabbi Jose brought a Bible and read aloud the statement about
Reuben and Bilha, and the story of Judah and Tamar. He said to her,
"See, if the Bible did not cover up the story of these men, why should
it cover up the story of Joseph? The very fact that it does not record
that Joseph sinned means that he remained innocent" (*Ber. Rab.* 87: 3,
6; *Mid. Tan.* Veyeshev).

*   *   *

The folklore about Joseph and his master's wife is full of human interest and finds parallels in other ancient literature. But we will be concerned here only with the argument raised by Rabbi Jose in his reply
to the Roman matron's question. Her incredulity at Joseph's self-
discipline was quite natural. We have to remember that her observation is made not from the background of Egyptian mores, but from
the context of Roman life. However immoral Egyptian society was,
Roman society was much worse. In the period of the Caesars Roman
behavior was notoriously profligate and the villas of the ruling class
were cesspools of debauchery, incest and gross immorality. It was
natural for the Roman lady to regard Joseph's behavior difficult to believe. Now Jose is not concerned here to criticize Mrs. Potiphar or to
denounce Roman immorality. He restricts himself to that point in the
Roman lady's question which casts doubt on the Bible's credibility.
Such things have never been heard before. The Bible must be covering up for one of its heroes.

The rabbi has a counter argument. The Bible, he says, does not
hide the sins of its heroes or sweep their failings under the carpet. It is
frank, honest and unashamedly blunt. When Judah goes to Tamar, his
daughter-in-law disguised as a harlot, the Bible tells us so. When
Reuben sleeps with Bilha, his own father's concubine, the Bible says
so in unmistakable language. In fact that incident is recorded in words

so few that they even deepen the disgust felt by the reader of the narrative. Of course Reuben was no great hero; but he was after all Jacob's firstborn, and he tried to save Joseph from the murderous intent of his brothers. Again, Judah is a gallant figure, the leader among Jacob's sons and destined to be the ancestor of the Davidic kingdom. Yet the Bible makes no attempt to hide their weaknesses and proves itself to be the impartial record of Israel's history. So Rabbi Jose argues that if it tells the truth about Reuben and Judah it is reasonable to hold that it tells the truth about Joseph. The Bible has no favorites and shows its impartiality even to the heroes of Jewish history.

Although Rabbi Jose's defence of the Bible is far from a scientific proof of the Bible's truth, and could hardly be accepted as an academic argument, it yet illustrates a remarkable characteristic of the biblical narrative and its unique approach to its great men. None of them is a superman. They are all human, with the natural failings and character weaknesses of ordinary people. So the Bible tells us that Abraham lied to the king of Egypt and the ruler of Gerar: so did Isaac under similar circumstances. They were strangers living in the territory ruled by those monarchs, and they let it be thought that their respective wives, Sarah and Rebekah, were not their wives but their sisters. Commentary and super-commentary notwithstanding, they admitted they they told those lies because they were afraid for their own lives; and they placed the matriarchs in great danger.

And what about Jacob? When he misrepresented himself to his old blind father, pretending to be Esau in order to obtain his father's parental blessing; it was flagrantly unethical by any standard of evaluation. It is true of course that in that incident, as well as in other incidents in the same category, some of the rabbinic commentaries are at pains to explain and absolve the conduct of the patriarchs. But their explanations are not too convincing and there is no doctrine on earth which says that we should accept them as anything but the overly pious attempts of some rabbis to make the patriarchs examples of the highest kind of moral beings. A more reasonable approach is to read the Bible record and to let it stand for what it is—a truthful and impartial account of the greatness and weakness of mortal man. The patriarchs are not angels. Incidentally, with regard to Jacob, his weak but all too human qualities are part of his popularity and his greatness. It is not what he was, but what he became which makes his story one of the most significant stories in the entire Bible. He started life as Jacob—literally 'the deceiver' and went on to become Israel—literally 'one who strives with God.'

Within the same context of the Bible's objectivity, we should mention the story of David's heinous offence with Bath-sheba. It is true that here again one can find a talmudic rabbi who will put up some kind of defence for David. But the defence is somewhat feeble and based on shaky historical and legal notions. More important for the Bible's moral evaluation of the story is the denunciation David received from the mouth of the prophet Nathan who delivered God's message of condemnation. Any oriental monarch of ancient times would have behaved as David did and would have escaped all censure. That was the right of kings. But not so in David's case, because of the Bible's clear pronouncement that even the king—perhaps especially the king—is subject to the higher law of God.

We may have travelled a little far from the central story of Joseph and Potiphar's wife, but our diversion led us to Rabbi Jose's observation that since the Bible does not hesitate to tell us of the sins of even its greatest characters, we have reason to believe that it certainly would have done the same had Joseph's behavior warranted it. Rabbi Jose's argument is that this supports the veracity of the biblical story of Joseph. In a wider sense it may support the belief in the objectivity and basic truth of the Bible.

ASPECTS OF JEWISH HISTORY

11

~

Why Was the Temple Destroyed?

In Jerusalem there lived a very wealthy and influential man who had a good friend named Kamtza, and an enemy named Bar Kamtza. One day this wealthy man made a big feast in honor of a family event, and as was customary he sent his servant to the homes of his friends and community leaders to invite them to his banquet. The servant went on his mission, but instead of inviting Kamtza, his master's friend, he invited Bar Kamtza, his master's enemy. When all the guests were assembled the host entered the dining hall, and looking around at his guests he was surprised to see Bar Kamtza among them.

"I want you to leave" he shouted angrily.

Bar Kamtza was embarrassed and said, "Let me remain here and I will pay you for what I eat."

"No you won't" said the man. "Go now."

"I will pay you the sum of half the banquet" said Bar Kamtza.

"I don't need your money" shouted the other, "I just want you to get out of here."

"If you let me stay" pleaded Bar Kamtza "I will pay for the entire banquet."

But the enraged host grew more angry and he rushed at Bar Kamtza and pushed him out of his house.

Now among the seated guests there were a number of distinguished rabbis and men of influence and leadership. They were all witnesses to the terrible scene, but remained silent.

Bar Kamtza felt hurt and humiliated. What pained him most—more than the cruel treatment of his enemy—was the silence of the rabbis and leaders. And he made up his mind that he would take his revenge against them. He went to a high officer of the Roman government and told them that the Jews were planning a rebellion against Rome. "What makes you think so?" asked the Roman. "It was something I overheard" answered Bar Kamtza "and I can prove it to you."

"How" asked the Roman official.

"All you have to do" said Bar Kamtza "is to send an animal to be sacrificed in the Jewish Temple in the name and in honor of the emperor. If they offer the sacrifice it will seem that they still honor the emperor. But if they reject the sacrifice you will have a clear sign of Jewish disrespect and of their rebellious intentions."

The Roman officer was satisfied with the suggestion and he had his people send an animal to the Temple to be offered as a sacrifice in honor of the emperor. But on the way, Bar Kamtza handled the animal on some pretext or other and managed to injure it with a very slight blemish of the kind that rendered it imperfect and therefore unfit for a sacrifice in the Temple.

The messengers arrived at the Temple gates and the animal was taken by the Temple officials and brought to the priests for examination. When they saw the slight blemish they sought the advice of the rabbis. In spite of the minor flaw some of them were in favor of allowing the sacrifice for the sake of peace and proper relations with the Roman emperor and authorities. But one of them, Zechariah ben Avkules, protested. "No" he insisted. "We cannot offer this animal for a sacrifice in case people get the impression that we are permitted to sacrifice a blemished animal. This is against the law." But then they were afraid that Bar Kamtza, who they guessed was behind all this, would tell the Roman authorities that the Jews had rejected a sacrifice sent to honor the emperor, and there could be serious danger for the Jews. There was even a suggestion that they have Bar Kamtza killed so that he would not cause further trouble. But Zechariah ben Avkules dissuaded them, again on a point of law, arguing that if they did that, people would get the false idea that anyone who maimed a sacrificial animal was liable to death.

So nothing was done. The animal was rejected and Bar Kamtza went back to the Roman official. "See" he said, "the Jews refuse to honor the emperor just as I told you they would." Soon after that, the Romans began their war against the Jews, and burned the Temple (*Git.* 55b–56a).

*   *   *

This well known story is part of a talmudic discussion on the question why the Temple was destroyed. In rabbinic theology, nothing happens just by chance. There is always a reason for what happens. And since God is the Lord of History, whatever happens takes place with his knowledge and in accordance with the divine dispensation of justice. The destruction of the Second Temple was a problem in rabbinic theology. The First Temple's destruction was easily explained. It was held that the First Temple, destroyed by the Babylonians in 586 B.C.E., was destroyed because of the sins of idolatry, sexual immorality and murder. These were the three heinous offences of which the people were guilty and for which they deserved destruction and exile. But the period of the Second Temple was entirely different. There was no idolatry and the people were innocent of the other two serious crimes. So why was the Second Temple destroyed? In the rabbinic system it must have happened because the people were guilty of other serious offences and deserved to be punished. There are many views expressed, which is an indication of the perceptive analysis of the rabbis when they examined the religious and social condition of their time. Here are just a few of the more insightful observations. The Temple was destroyed because of the negligence of the people in their failure to read the *Shema* twice a day (disregard of regular prayer). The Temple was destroyed because the children failed to attend schools to study Torah (lack of Jewish education). The Temple was destroyed because of the blatant shamelessness of the people (unabashed and brazen-faced even when guilty of wrongdoing). The Temple was destroyed because of lack of honest leadership. The Temple was destroyed because the rabbis judged in accordance with the strictest letter of the law and failed to bend a little to inform their decisions with more compassion for the needy (*Shab.* 119b; *B. Metz.* 30b).

But the most widespread view held that the Temple was destroyed because of *sinat hinam*, causeless hatred. At the time of the Roman wars the people were fragmented into several parties, from the aggressive and militant zealots on the right to the rabbinic groups who advocated peace with the Romans. But the divisions were not only expressed in the political life of the people. They were also divided religiously among the Pharisee party of the rabbis, the Sadducees of the wealthy and priestly families and the Essenes who removed themselves altogether from the mainstream of the community and went to live their own secluded life in the area of the Dead Sea. These divisions and cross divisions were more than enough to splinter the community into many troublesome and antagonistic groups. But in addition, there existed at that time the poisonous element of personal hatred among individuals. This is the *sinat hinam* which is illustrated in our story and which rabbis of a later generation blamed for the destruction of the Temple. The authors of this viewpoint were sensitive enough to recognize that the social evil of *sinat hinam* was a cancer in the life of the community which destroyed any possibility of survival in the face of the Roman threat to the Jewish people. In their characteristically quaint way they submitted their social message in the form of the story told above, prefacing their narrative with the statement that the Temple was destroyed because of Kamtza and Bar Kamtza.

But the careful reader will recognize that we have here another lesson which derives from the character and opinions of Zechariah ben Avkilus.

There have always been halakhic authorities who insisted that whatever the circumstances, the strictest letter of the law must be enforced. The cry, *Yikov ha-din et ha-har* (*San.* 6b), "Let the law split the mountain" if it must; the law has to be enforced as the supreme value. Such an uncompromising view may have acted as a safeguard for the preservation of the law—although even that is doubtful. What is certain however, is that in adopting such a stringent and unbending policy innocent individuals have frequently been hurt because they were caught up in a situation where the applied halakhah could not be interpreted in their favor. The case of an unfortunate wife who is refused a divorce by a blackmailing husband is only one case in point. The result of such a policy has left many thousands of deserted wives without help. The problem is still with us. But our story relates to the situation of the Roman-Jewish confrontation. It is more than likely that the Romans would have seized Jerusalem even without the strictures of Zechariah ben Avkilus. However, the point made in our story was that it was quite unnecessary to give the Romans an excuse for the attack by implying a clear insult to the Roman emperor. At least that is how the Romans would have interpreted the rejection of the royal sacrifice. And what was the reason for the rejection? A slight defect in the animal which was so tiny that it could hardly be seen. Indeed, there were some scholars in that consultation who advised accepting the sacrifice. In any case, they argued, the value of peace was involved. And peace is the greater value than the minute point of the halakhah of animal sacrifices. For peace saves human life. That is why one rabbinic view has the interesting view that it was the over-scrupulousness of Zechariah ben Avkilus which brought about the destruction of the Temple.

12

The Eternal Jew

When Pharaoh decreed that every male child born to the Hebrews should be thrown into the River Nile, the Hebrew mothers tried every expedient and ploy to save their children. Some managed by hiding them in cellars or in other out-of-the-way places where it would be difficult for the children to be found. In that way quite a number of Hebrew babies were saved. But in time the Egyptians became suspicious of what was going on, so when they saw the Hebrew woman about to give birth they would report the birth to the Egyptian soldiers. But when the soldiers made a search of the Hebrew houses the infants were nowhere to be found. So the cruel Egyptians hit upon a plan. On learning of the birth of a Hebrew baby, they would visit the house bringing their own babies with them. On arriving at the Hebrew house they would pinch their own infants who would naturally set up a loud wailing. The Hebrew babes would hear the crying and of course would then join in from wherever they had been hidden. In that way the male children of the Hebrews would be discovered and taken away by the Egyptian officers to be drowned.

God then said to his angels, "Go down and see how the children of my beloved Abraham, Isaac and Jacob are being drowned in the river." The angels went down and were appalled to see what was happening. They determined to save the children and waded into the river. They caught the infants in their arms and placed them safely in the crevices of the rocks which jutted out of the water. God also provided nipples in the rocks and the babies sucked honey water and other nourishment (*Sh. Ha-Sh. Rab.* 2; *Tan. Db' El.* 8).

*   *   *

Taking the biblical account of the drowning of the Israelite children as historically true, the rabbis had a problem. If every male child born to the Hebrews was drowned, how was it possible that at the Exodus—say eighty years later—the Bible can record that six hundred thousand adult males left Egyptian bondage?

Of course, there are several possibilities here. First, that the extermination by drowning did not last too long. Second, that the Egyptians were selective in carrying out that order since in any case it was important for them to maintain the strength of the free labor force available to them from the masses of Hebrew slaves. And third, one can assume that every parent would have tried to find ways and means to save their children. This happened, for example, with Moses, who was hidden by his mother for three months.

But the probability is that the midrashic authors are not interested in answering questions of history. They are more interested in theology and their story is rooted in the doctrine of divine providence, and their unshakeable belief in the indestructibility of the Jewish people. In spite of everything that could happen to the Jews there was a divine plan at work which mysteriously keeps Israel alive. The words of Isaiah are full of meaning in the context of such a belief, *No weapon that is formed against thee shall prosper* . . . (Isa. 54:17). It is a teaching which is repeated again and again in the prophetic messages. God loves Israel. He promised the patriarchs that their descendants would become a great nation, living in peace and security, and that His covenant with Israel would endure. The grim realities of Jewish life under Rome made it difficult to hold on to this doctrine. Nevertheless the rabbis insisted in maintaining its centrality in the difficult and dark age of the Roman oppression and exile. They couldn't explain the workings of God or answer the questions raised by Jewish suffering. Yet they had the tradition to strengthen them, and that tradition encouraged their belief that divine providence will protect the Jews even as it has kept them alive until their day.

If the story of the miraculous survival of the Hebrew infants symbolized the subsequent survival of the Jewish people, then it served the rabbis of the Midrash. They had lived through the latest crisis—the destruction of the Second Temple. But it was not only the

Temple which had been destroyed. Many hundreds of thousands of Jews had died by the sword or starvation, and many more had left the Holy Land to add substantially to the growing dispersal of the Jews. An objective historian would have written that the year 70 C.E. with the demise of the second Jewish Commonwealth and the destruction of the Temple, followed by the disastrous failure of the Bar Kokhba rebellion sixty years or so later, marked the end of the history of the Jewish people. Yet it didn't. It marked rather the beginning of a new volume. The story of the Jews continued; but with new directions. For the rabbinic mind it still seemed that the watchful providence of God remained unbroken, and that God still remained faithful to His divine promise for the eternity of Israel.

And that same doctrine can be extended to meet later and modern periods of Jewish history, including the Holocaust, when more than one third of the entire Jewish people was murdered, including more than a million children who were not saved by the angels.

Now of course, the rabbis rarely rationalized the doctrine of divine providence: mostly they taught it as a straight principle of faith. Even later historians have done little more than state the facts of the ups and downs, the waxings and the wanings in Jewish history. The finger of God, and the way and why it moved could not be explained.

Yet when we write on this theme in our time, we cannot avoid an attempt at some rationalization, however partial or even simplistic. Granted that most Jewish theologians do not explain the ways of God which cannot be understood, nor His purpose which cannot be fathomed, yet a historian these days can and does try to explain the facts of history. Here we will just quote, by way of example, the words of the famous Jewish historian Heinrich Graetz (1817–1891) who wrote as follows: "What has prevented this constantly migrating people, this veritable wandering Jew, from degenerating into brutalized vagabonds, into vagrant hordes of Gypsies? The answer is at hand. In its journey through the desert of life, for eighteen centuries, the Jewish people carried along the Ark of the Covenant, which breathed into its heart ideal aspirations, and even illuminated the badge of disgrace affixed to its garment. . . . The prescribed, outlawed and universally persecuted Jew, felt a sublime, noble pride in being singled out to perpetuate and to suffer for a religion which reflects eternity . . . and which is on that very account eternal."

In other words, it came down to a question of spiritual survival. Nothing can destroy a faith, an idea, a truth. That is eternal. And so long as there were Jews who remained loyal to the Torah and their faith, then Judaism could survive, and the Jews who kept firm to it remained unsubmerged and distinctive. Of course millions were murdered in the struggle for survival and over the numerous centuries many millions more were drowned in the depths of assimilation. But at the same time millions managed to keep their heads above the threatening waters, and they and their descendants lived on to prove the validity of the doctrine of the mysterious providence of God which is linked to the equally profound mystery of the eternal Jew.

13

~

And the Letters Fly Upward

One day the Romans came upon Hananiah ben Teradyon holding a scroll of the Law from which he was teaching a group of his disciples. This had been strictly forbidden by the Romans on penalty of death, so they immediately arrested him. He was sentenced to be burned at the stake, his wife to be executed, and a daughter to be sold to a brothel. Hananiah was tied up and the scroll of the Torah with which he had been caught was wrapped around his body. In order to prolong his death the Romans placed against his heart pads of wool soaked in water to prevent him dying too quickly.

As the flames reached up to the sage, family and friends watched the awesome sight.

"Father, say something to us" said his daughter.

"If I were being executed on my own I would have been sadder" said the martyred sage. "But now that God's Torah burns together with me, I know that He who will avenge the destruction of the Torah will also avenge my death."

His disciples came forward and asked, "Master, what do you see?"

Hananiah replied, "I see the Torah parchment burning, but the letters are flying up to heaven."

As the rabbi suffered his slow and agonizing death, the Roman executioner approached and said, "If I remove the wool and increase the flames to enable you to die quicker, will I enter the World to Come?"

"Yes" whispered the rabbi.

"Promise me" begged the Roman. And the rabbi promised.

Whereupon the executioner removed the wool pads, and increased the fuel to make a huge blaze. Hananiah's death came in moments, and as the flames reached their peak the Roman executioner threw himself into the pyre and perished with the rabbi. A heavenly voice was heard to say, "Hananiah and his executioner have both entered the World to Come" (*Av. Zar.* 17b–18a).

*   *   *

In the terrible persecutions which befell the Jews in the Hadrianic period after the abortive Bar Kokhba revolt, the Romans not only prohibited the practice of Judaism and the teaching of Torah, but they cruelly put to death many rabbinic leaders of the time who were caught in acts of disobedience against the Roman edict. The story of the martyred Hananiah is found in several rabbinic sources. Outside the Talmud the best known of those sources is the Midrash of the Ten Martyrs, which forms the basis for the martyrology section of the Yom Kippur Musaf Service, known by its title, *Asarah Harugei Malkhut*. There the story teller brings together the martyrdom of the ten most famous rabbinic leaders who lived at the end of the first and during the second centuries. There may not be any historical basis for the midrashic-liturgical account. Nevertheless it is essentially true to the historical background of the times, as well as to the record of the many sacrifices made by Israel's leadership who accepted death by execution as the price they were willing to pay for their part in preserving Judaism.

Hananiah's martyrdom is particularly grim. But it is distinctive in two respects. First, in the self-execution of the Roman, followed by the heavenly announcement that he had entered the World to Come together with Hananiah. The Roman was a simple pagan who earned his immortal reward at the very end of his life. He achieved his portion in the World to Come not by jumping into the fire, since his place in paradise had been promised by Hananiah before that. He earned it by speeding up the death of the sage and diminishing his agony—an act motivated by some compassion.

But the chief lesson of the story is in Hananiah's reply to the question of his disciples, "What do you see?" The rabbi answered, "I see the parchment burning but the letters are flying up to heaven." The dying Hananiah can perhaps see more than ordinary people in the midst of life. That is why the disciples asked him what he sees;

what special vision or spiritual truth does he experience. And the rabbi's reply is full of profound meaning. It is couched in rather mystical language, but it points to the significant fact of Jewish existence.

The "Torah parchment" represents the physical part of Jewish life. The "letters" themselves are the spiritual life. What Hananiah is saying is that the physical body of the Jewish people may be tortured and even killed, but Israel's spiritual life is indestructible and cannot be touched by the flames.

It is here suggested that this is a kind of flash photograph of Jewish history. Entire Jewish communities have been destroyed and Jewish lives have been brutally and mercilessly exterminated. The Babylonian exile, the Roman oppression, the Crusades, the Inquisition, banishments and the Holocaust have been recurring themes in the Jewish record. No other people has had to bear so much suffering as the Jews have borne during two thousand years of exile. And yet, what was destroyed is like the parchment of the Torah—the physical and material life of communities and of countless individuals. But the Torah letters flew upward. That is, the essence of Jewish spiritual life remained alive and even flourished. Miraculously it was preserved to reunite again with Jewish people in other countries and at other times. If the story of Israel's wanderings covers the globe, so does the story of the transmigration of the faith. Wherever Jews lived they picked up elements of their spiritual life. Babylon produced the Talmud, Spain produced the philosophies and the poetry, Eastern Europe contributed talmudic thoroughness and Western Europe gave us Jewish scientific scholarship. There were many times when the physical body was destroyed, but the holy letters of the spiritual life always survived. Because they were indestructible the Jewish people itself survived. That is what Hananiah was saying with his dying words. And the message seems to provide the clue to an understanding of the past.

14

~

The Roots of Antisemitism

Rav and Samuel, two third century Babylonian teachers, debated the roots of antisemitism. The famous discussion centered around the meaning of the biblical verse, *Now a new king arose over Egypt who knew not Joseph* (Ex. 1:8). One of them favoured the historical approach. "Yes" he said, "the new king was the founder of a new revolutionary dynasty, and when the Bible states that he knew not Joseph it means just that. He came with a new policy towards the Hebrews and he was quite unconcerned with the life-saving contribution of Joseph to the masses of Egyptians during the years of famine." His colleague however thought otherwise and suggested that it was the very same king who had been friendly to Joseph and his family, and who now changed his policy. The phrase *who knew not Joseph* simply means that through his new policy he made it seem as if he did not know Joseph. Circumstances changed. The political climate became problematical. There were new elements and dangers on the international horizon. And his earlier benevolent policy toward the descendants of the former savior of Egypt and his family changed overnight in order to meet the new conditions of the political scene.

Other rabbis seem to support this view but offer some explanation by suggesting that the Egyptian king was forced by the ignorant mob to change his policy towards the Hebrews. They picture what happened in this way. For some years after the time of Joseph, the Hebrews in Egypt multiplied and prospered. Then Egyptian mobs came to the king and said, "Let us exploit the Hebrews and make them our forced slaves!" We can imagine that they had cast an envious and greedy eye on the large and prosperous Hebrew settlement. But Pharaoh's initial response to them was clear and he replied, "You fools! For many years we have been enjoying prosperity only because of Joseph's wisdom and dedication to Egypt. Had it not been for him we would have all been dead! So how can you possibly want to harm the family of this man?" But the street mobs and hooligans were not persuaded, and they managed to engineer a palace revolt which deposed Pharaoh for three months. After that time the king gave in to their demands and the new policy of Hebrew enslavement was decreed.

But even this does not exhaust the interesting rabbinic discussion. Some rabbis go off on an entirely different tangent and suggest that it was the Hebrews themselves who knew not Joseph. Of course this is not what the Bible says. But this rabbinic comment attempts to explore the theology behind the persecution. They said, It has nothing to do with politics. It was punishment because the Hebrews began to assimilate. When Joseph died the old patriarchal influence disappeared from Hebrew life, and they said, "We want to be just like the Egyptians!" They even ceased to practice the basic Hebrew rite of circumcision. Consequently God reversed the Egyptians' early friendship for the Hebrews and turned it into hatred (*Ex. Rab.* 1; *Sot.* 11a).

*   *   *

It is not difficult to find here elements of the modern debate on the root causes of antisemitism. The first rabbi would say that the situation of the Jewish minority in its host country is always precarious. Nothing is guaranteed. Regimes come and go, and antisemitism can easily become the official policy of a new set of rulers for any one of a variety of reasons which suits them and their new national policy. In that case the earlier and more friendly policies of the former regimes, which the Jews might have enjoyed for centuries, are swept away in new revolutionary fervor. It doesn't matter how long the Jews had been settled in the country. Nor is any significance attached to the contributions the Jews may have made to the economic prosperity and the cultural advancement of their country of adoption. New governments introduce new policies, and the situation of the Jews is of little concern. See what happened, for example, in Germany, where the contribution of the Jews in the fields of science, the arts, philanthropy, education and economics had been enormous. Yet the Nazi rulers turned against the Jews as their first and most acceptable target, and ruthlessly wiped out two out of every three European Jews.

The second view is also borne out by the facts of modern history. The same king, the same regime can also have a change of policy towards the Jews any time it wants to—if its own national interests are involved. After 1967, France adopted a new and unfriendly attitude toward Israel. After 1973, other European and African countries became more and more pro-Arab and more and more anti-Israel, because of their concern to safeguard their vital oil supplies from Arab oil-producing countries. A larger number of countries also subscribed, wholly or partially, to the rules of the Arab boycott against economic relations with Israel. In the arena of world politics and economics the Jews and Israel are easily expendable since the oil-soaked countries with their dominating financial position can virtually call the tune to which oil-starved countries have to dance.

Then the supplementary picture of the ignorant, greedy and lawless mob also carries with it elements which are painfully recognizable. Mob lawlessness inflamed the crowds, sending them into a frenzy of murder, destruction and looting during the Chmielnicki massacres in seventeenth-century Poland, the pogroms in nineteenth-century Russia, and in twentieth-century Nazi Germany.

Of greater difficulty to the modern mind is the implication of the final observation of some teachers where it appears that they connect the antisemitism and persecution of the Jews in some countries to a deeper theological belief. The discussion is then taken out of the area of politics and set within the framework of religious doctrine. According to this view, nothing happens without God allowing it to happen. And when something bad happens to the Jews it is to test them, or to punish them for being disloyal to God's law. For example, this school of rabbinic thought held that the Jews of Persia in the fifth century B.C.E. were put to the severe test of threatened extermination, as described in the Book of Esther, because they were on the road to assimilation. It should be added that this view is not supported by other rabbis who actually give credit to the Jews of Persia for their loyalty to their faith. But it is certain that this "punishment" school of theology has maintained its place in classical Jewish thought. It is perhaps encapsulated in the liturgical phrase, *U-Mipne Hataenu Galinu Me-Artzenu*, "For our sins we have been exiled from our land." We will not discuss here the hard problem involved in such a theory. It is sufficient for our present purpose that we have brought together four opinions dealing with the causes of antisemitism—an old and modern problem.

We can conclude this piece with one further note. In the modern debate, there is still no consensus on the matter. Is antisemitism caused perhaps by Jewish wealth which excites the envy and greed of the mob? Then look at pre-War antisemitic Poland, where the masses of the Jews were huddled together in pitiful poverty. Or is the antisemite attracted to the Jews because they are poor, defenceless and powerless, then look at Nazi Germany, where the Jews constituted a large upper middle class community, highly competent and not without some influence. Is antisemitism the result of Church doctrine? Then turn to atheistic Soviet Russia where anti-Jewish feeling and antisemitic policy were very strong. Does antisemitism breed in ignorance? Then take another look at Germany, a nation that had the reputation of being one of the most educationally advanced and culturally sophisticated countries in the world. Or perhaps antisemitism is nurtured precisely in academia? Then what about the backward countries of the Third World and the anti-Jewish riots of the ignorant frenzied mobs in Eastern Europe!

The probable truth of the matter is that it is impossible to identify a single cause for antisemitism. It is rather a phenomenon deriving from an accumulation of multiple factors—economic, political, educational, religious and psychological. At any one time, a situation can arise in any country where a combination of adverse factors will threaten the position of a minority, and particularly the traditional minority—the Jews.

In the result the Jews of our time have to make one of two choices. Either they learn to live with the risks, the hidden fears and the uncertainty. Or they can decide to live in Israel where they have the chance to be rid of all those fears and dangers. True, even if they make the second choice, there is a problem of security also in Israel. But it is not the problem of classical antisemitism. It is rather the problem of free men living as part of a free nation struggling to preserve their security and their independence in their very own country.

15

~

In Spite of Everything

When Abraham started on his journey with Isaac to obey God's command to sacrifice his son, Satan disguised himself as an old man and accosted the patriarch.

"Where are you going?" asked Satan.

"To pray" answered Abraham.

"Then why on earth are you carrying wood and a knife?"

"Well" answered Abraham, "in case we decide to camp out for a day or two and we will need to cook and bake."

"Old man" said Satan, "I want you to know that I was present when God told you to slaughter your son, and I think you've lost your mind. Here you are at the age of one hundred. At last you have the son you have been waiting for, and you are ready to kill him!"

"Yes, I am" answered Abraham quietly. "For that is what God requires of me."

"And what if God continues to make more difficult demands?" asked Satan.

"However much I am tested, and whatever the demands, I will be ready" Abraham affirmed.

"And what if God asks you tomorrow to kill yourself because you killed your son?" persisted Satan. "What will you do then?"

"I will still carry out His command" said Abraham.

Seeing that he got nowhere with Abraham, Satan tried with Isaac. First he changed himself into a youngster, and he stood before Isaac.

"Where are you going?" he asked.

"To study Torah" answered Isaac.

"Before your death or after it" taunted Satan.

"Can anyone study Torah after his death?" asked the youngster.

"Alas! you poor boy! I am pained when I think of your pitiful mother! How many fasts she kept and how many prayers she offered before you were born. And now this fool of an old man, your father, is on his way to slaughter you!"

"Just the same" said Isaac "I will not rebel against the will of God or against the decision of my father."

When Satan saw that he was getting nowhere with either of them, he changed himself into a wide river in order to prevent them crossing over on their journey. Abraham immediately walked into the river and when the water reached to his knees he instructed Isaac and his servants to follow him. But then the water got deeper and deeper and when it reached his neck he looked up to heaven and prayed, "O God, You chose me: You revealed Yourself to me and said, 'I am the One and you are the one, and through you My Name shall be acknowledged throughout the world. Now go and offer up Isaac as a burned offering.' I did not demur and I am now on my way to carry out Your command. But the waters of this river are now set to take away my life. If I or my son Isaac drown then who will carry out Your commands and who will proclaim You as the Only One God?"

Immediately, God rebuked the river which then disappeared leaving Abraham and his company to proceed on dry ground. When they finally arrived at the prescribed place for the sacrifice, Abraham and Isaac got everything ready. Abraham built the altar and secured Isaac on it. The eyes of the father were on the eyes of the son, and the eyes of the son were on the innermost heavens. Abraham's tears flowed down his whole face as he took up the knife to slaughter his son. At that very moment Satan intervened again, and pushed Abraham's hand so that the patriarch dropped the knife. To the very end Satan was determined to stop Abraham from proving his faith in God. But the patriarch picked up the knife and went to perform the slaughter. Abraham had passed the test of faith.

But it was not part of God's plan that Isaac should be sacrificed. Rows and rows of angels in the heavens above cried out to God to have Him immediately stop the sacrifice, and God despatched the angel Michael to prevent Abraham from killing his son (*San.* 89b; *Pirke D'Rab. El.* 31; *Yal. Vayera*).

*   *   *

The story of the binding of Isaac (Gen. 22) is a biblical episode which has been interpreted more than any other story of the Bible. There are well over one hundred thousand commentaries, interpretations, essays and books written about this story in almost every language. Moreover, in the course of time it became a great watershed of theological discussion.

In Jewish literature the main treatment of the story elevates Abraham as the model of total and unquestioned faith in God. The patriarch is ready to do whatever he believes is God's will, even if the divine command seems to be beyond all reason. Whatever the cost, Abraham is ready to carry it out because his faith is so strong and immovable.

However, the rabbinic treatment of the subject is also involved in examining the story from different aspects. The treatment in the above midrashic selection uses the story of the binding of Isaac as a symbol of Jewish history, with all its difficult situations, impossible demands bloodshed and self-sacrifice. In all this, the facts of Jewish life have been cruel enough to destroy Israel's faith in God. It is as if the command *Take now thy son, thine only son whom thou lovest . . . and offer him for a burnt offering* has been the constant reality which has re-echoed again and again during the epochs of Jewish history. Under those bitter conditions the Jews might have given up and lost their faith and abdicated their place in history. The Satan in the above legend tries everything with one purpose—to prevent Abraham from carrying out what the patriarch believes is God's will and in that way to sever the nexus of faith which binds Abraham to God. He symbolizes the cruel historical forces which were more than enough to break the loyalty of the Jew and to turn him away from God. But in spite of all, the Jew has walked through the fires of his history with his determination and his faith unimpaired.

The rabbis wove their tales under the conditions of Roman oppression and exile, so they experienced the symbolism of the binding of Isaac as a reality in their own lives. Similar religious-historical evaluations were made by writers throughout the darkness of the middle ages. The medieval chronicler Solomon Ibn Vega tells the story of a Jewish family, exiles from the Spanish expulsion of 1492, who paid their way on a boat where the captain was to take them to another country. However the rapacious master of the ship took them to an isolated desert island and then left with his boat. The man, his wife and two young children trekked through the arid waste without food or water. The woman died, and after burying her the man walked on with his children until the elder son also died for lack of water. The grief stricken father carried his remaining child on his back and struggled on in the hope that they would be seen by a passing ship. But in a few hours his second child died. The man buried the dead boy and then stood up and proclaimed, "O God! You seem to be doing everything You can to make me lose my faith in You. But know that whatever You do, and whatever You may do in the future, I will never reject my faith in You and in Your ultimate mercy!" So saying he pronounced the words of the kaddish, *Yitgadal, ve'yitkadash Shemei Rabah*—'Magnified and hallowed be the Name of the Most High.' Some hours later a passing ship stopped at the island and took the man to safety where he was able to tell his story.

In modern times, the tragic experiences of the Jews in the Holocaust made the binding of Isaac story and all subsequent and similar experiences real, painful events. But in spite of all, the Jew has held fast to his faith in God; and with that faith he has lived on until he has reached the new age of redemption.

16

~

The Great Coffin Escape

The leading rabbinic authority and head of the Great Sanhedrin in Jerusalem in the days before the destruction of the Second Temple in the year 70 C.E. was Rabbi Johanan ben Zakkai. When that sage realised that the end was imminent he sent a message to his nephew, Abba Sikra, who was the head of the fanatical gang of extremists in their fight against Rome, and asked him to come to him secretly.

When Abba Sikra arrived, Johanan said to him, "How much longer are you going to hold out in this hopeless struggle and starve the people to death?"

"What can I do?" replied Abba Sikra. "If I had made any attempt to stop my men from burning down the granaries they would have killed me."

The rabbi thought for a while and then said to his visitor, "I have to get out of Jerusalem somehow to try to save something of the situation. Now your guards are at the city gates and will not permit anyone to leave. I want you to work out a plan by which I will be able to leave the city. Perhaps there is something I can do."

It didn't take Abba Sikra too long to come up with a scheme. "I suggest that you spread a rumor that you are very sick and near to death. Then let word get around that you have died, and two of your disciples will carry your bier out of the city for 'burial.'"

Johanan accepted the idea and everything went according to plan, with Rabbis Joshua and Eliezer carrying the bier on which lay the covered body of their master. Then when they reached the city gates the mournful procession was challenged by the guards. "What have you there?" they demanded. "It is the body of our deceased master" they replied. The guards were suspicious and one of them said, "We will test your report and pierce the body through with our swords." The disciples protested in horror. "No!" they cried. "How can you desecrate the pure body of our master?"

"Then we will throw the bier over the walls on to the other side" they said. "But how can you do such a thing?" the escorting rabbis pleaded. "Even the Romans would hold us in greater derision for such a deed."

Finally they were allowed through the gate, and when they were safely away, Rabbi Johanan ben Zakkai got on his feet and made his way to the Roman camp commanded by Vespasian.

When the rabbi was admitted to Vespasian's tent he greeted the Roman, "Hail to thee! O emperor!"

The Roman general was astonished at this and said, "You have committed two offences for which you could be put to death. First of all, I am not the emperor. Second that you did not come to see me before this."

Rabbi Johanan answered, "I could not come before because of the city defenders who let no one leave. And as for my calling you "emperor" that is true because the last emperor is now dead and the leaders in Rome have proclaimed you the new emperor."

Just then official couriers arrived in the camp and reported to Vespian that he had been officially proclaimed in Rome as the new emperor.

The Roman and the rabbi continued their discussion for a little while longer in the course of which Vespian became impressed with the rabbi's wisdom and perceptiveness. "I am leaving now" he said, and I will send someone else to continue here. But before I go I offer you three requests. Ask and it shall be done."

When Rabbi Johanan heard this, he knew that his chance had come to achieve something important. "Spare Jabneh and its wise men. Spare the family of Rabbi Gamaliel. Send physicians to cure Rabbi Zadok" (*Git.* 56a–b).

*   *   *

This well known story is found in several rabbinic sources, in addition to the one given above, and its multiple sources, as well as its central idea having its place in the histories, is an indication of the importance writers have attached to its meaning. But first of all, one or two introductory points will be in order.

The Jewish war against the Romans (66–73 C.E.) was spurred on by the Zealots, a strongly nationalistic and armed group who were generally supported by the people as a whole. A splinter group of Zealots was the Sicarii, a name which comes from the Latin meaning "a short curved dagger" which was carried by these men under their cloaks and with which they attacked not only Romans but Jews whom they accused of being collaborators with the Romans. The Sicarii sealed off Jerusalem and would not permit anyone to leave during the siege. Worse, they are supposed to have burned down the storage houses and granaries in Jerusalem, presumably in a wild attempt to harden a feeling of desperate resistance among the people. Josephus, and others, wrote about the Sicarii in terms of disgust, while there are some historians who lay the burden of blame for the destruction of Jerusalem and the Temple at the door of the Sicarii extremists.

Vespian was the emperor of Rome from 69 until 79. His real predecessor was Nero who died in 68. In the interval Rome was in a chaotic state with several leaders who reigned very briefly. The last of them was Vitellius Aulus who was killed. Vespian was first hailed as emperor by the forces in Egypt, then by the army in Judea, and finally in Rome.

Now for the real lesson of the story. Johanan ben Zakkai was no prophet. But he was a keen student of history and was possessed of remarkable perception with the gift of understanding the political realities of the day. His greeting to Vespian could be interpreted in that light. But more significant was his escape from Jerusalem and his requests to the Roman leader. He knew that the Jewish war against Rome was doomed to failure. It had been hopeless from the start, and as the massive might of Rome was turned in full force against Judea, it became obvious that in a short while the Jews would have no state of their own; they would lose all independence; and even the Temple might be destroyed.

Now without a land, without a Temple and without political independence, how could the Jewish people survive? More especially, how could Judaism survive? Johanan had one answer, and that was that Judaism does not rest on a land or on a Temple. It rests on the spread of a knowledge and observance of Torah law and teaching. The centrality of Torah had to take the place of land and Temple; the rabbis had to replace the priests, and observance and piety had to replace sacrifices. When Johanan asked for Jabneh and its sages he asked for the chance to preserve the Torah knowledge and the rabbinic center of authority.

Many years later, there were some teachers who criticized Rabbi Johanan for not asking for much more. He might have even been able to persuade Vespian to leave Jerusalem alone. But Johanan was too much of a realist. He knew that he could not overplay his hand by excessive demands. And he knew that if he only secured his academy and the safety of the sages in Jabneh then Judaism would be safe. If Judaism was safe then there would be a future for the Jews. The Roman did not know that in acceding to Johanan's request he guaranteed the survival of the Jewish people.

17

~

The Silence of God

Commenting on the well-known verse . . . *The voice of thy brother's blood crieth unto Me from the ground* (Gen. 4:10) Rabbi Simeon bar Yohai said, "I find what I have to say very difficult, but in spite of that I feel I have to say it. The matter can be compared to the case of two gladiators fighting to the death in the arena. Finally, one gladiator gets the better of the fight, and he is about to run his sword through his victim. Before doing so however, he looks up to the emperor who is sitting in the royal seat watching the bloody contest. Everyone knows that if the emperor shows the 'thumbs down' signal the the victor has the royal assent to kill his victim. But if the emperor shows the 'thumbs up' then the victim is spared. As the gladiators look up to the emperor, the Roman ruler who has the fate of the unfortunate loser literally in his hands shows the sign of condemnation. Then before he is slain the victim calls out to the emperor, 'Had thou wished you could have spared me: now my blood will cry out accusing you of my murder!' (*Ber. Rab.* 22:9).

*   *   *

It is clear that in the above rabbinic parable Cain and Abel symbolize Rome and the Jews, and Abel's death symbolizes the destruction of the Temple and Jerusalem, the slaughter of numerous Jews and the suffering of the survivors under the cruel oppression of the Romans. Simeon bar Yohai, the author of the above midrash lived in the second century, during the Bar Kokhba rebellion and the subsequent severe persecution of the Jews by Emperor Hadrian. He was an outspoken and fearless critic of the Romans, on account of which he had to flee for his life when they sentenced him to death. In our present midrash he shows another example of his outspokenness; but this time in criticism of God for His silence in the face of Jewish suffering. He does not follow the traditional line that Jewish suffering is the result of sin for which they are punished. Nor does he go along with any of the other rabbinic theories or reactions to national tragedy. He can be said to be the author of "The First Holocaust Midrash" since he wants to know why God is silent. More than that he seems to accuse God for permitting the oppression and the slaughter of His people, since if He had so willed it, He could have saved the Jews. But, like the emperor in our story, He gave the "thumbs down" signal, and untold numbers of Jews were slain.

Of course, what Simeon bar Yohai says is daring and unorthodox. And Simeon knows it. That is why he apologizes for what he is about to say. On the other hand, it is not heretical, because it could have been said only by someone who had a total belief in God's omnipotence and His goodness. He does not question those tenets of his faith. His criticism of God arises precisely because he believes in God's omnipotence and goodness. It is his cry of anguish, wanting to understand the ways of God. Meanwhile, Simeon's question remains unanswered. God is silent and the rabbi cannot understand why this is so. And it remains the big question in all theistic faiths. As far as the Jewish question is concerned it was left to other teachers to attempt other answers to Jewish suffering. Nevertheless, within the totality of reactions to the national tragedy which are found in rabbinic literature, Simeon's extreme and untypical reaction is worthy of note.

18

The Weeping God

Rabbi Jose told the following story. "One day I was walking in Jerusalem when it was time for the evening prayer, so I turned off the road and went into one of the city ruins to pray. In the middle of my devotions the prophet Elijah arrived and stood at the entrance of the ruin until I finished my prayers. When I came out he greeted me.

"Peace to you, my master" he said.

"Peace to you my master and teacher" I returned.

"My child, what are you doing here?" he asked.

"I went inside to pray."

"But you could have prayed out on the road" he said.

"I was afraid that I might be disturbed" I replied.

Elijah wanted to know more about my religious experience praying inside the ruin of the holy city.

"Did you hear anything extraordinary?" he asked me.

"Yes, I did" I answered. "I heard a heavenly sound, like that of a crying dove, and it seemed to say, 'Woe is me that I have destroyed My house, burned My Temple and sent My children into exile among the nations.'"

Elijah then said to me, "I swear that such a divine lament is heard not just once; but three times every day God mourns like that . . ." (*Ber.* 3a).

* * *

After the destruction of the Second Temple by the Romans in the years 70 C.E., other cities took the place of Jerusalem as the center of Jewish learning, and the seat of rabbinic authority moved from one place to another. In time the focus of religious leadership was located in the north, in the Galilee. One of the chief towns in that district was Sepphoris, not far from Haifa, on the central plain. That place was the home town of a sage named Jose ben Halafta.

Jose was one of the last disciples of the martyred Rabbi Akiba, and like his great teacher he risked his life to preserve Judaism in the face of the prohibitions of the Romans, particularly after the defeat of Bar Kokhba in 135. Jose was a great scholar and his contemporary, Judah the Prince, who later codified the Mishnah, frequently incorporated Jose's views in his code.

Now Jose had an additional claim to fame, and that is that he was frequently visited by the prophet Elijah—none else. Of course there were other rabbis of whom it is said that they were visited by and had spoken to the spirit of Elijah. In fact, by itself that does not seem to have been so remarkable. The time was ripe for mystical speculation, particularly when the grim situation of the real world was so hard to bear and the future seemed bleak and hopeless. In periods of national depression sensitive spirits often took refuge in mysticism, in notions of the spiritual world where all is truth and suffering is no more; and especially in their visionary dreams of the Messiah and his forerunner Elijah the prophet, the messenger of God.

But there was something unique about Jose's meetings with Elijah. That was their regularity. Other teachers might have a vision of the prophet once or twice, or at odd times. In the case of Rabbi Jose, however, it is said that during one period of his life the prophet visited him every day, and when he missed for three days running the rabbi became really upset.

The spiritual-mystical phenomenon involved in the experience of some rabbis to commune with Elijah the prophet will not be our concern here. At this point what we are chiefly interested in is Jose's report and Elijah's comment on God's own lament for the destruction of Jerusalem and the Temple.

The central problem for religious faith is why God allows suffering. Either He is not all-good and therefore permits it, or He is not all-powerful and therefore can do nothing about it. Judaism however holds that God is both all-good and all-powerful. In the many centuries of theological probings there have hardly been more than one or two significant philosophers who compromised with any part of that theological position. So the problem remains. And it is all the more difficult in relation to the destruction of the Temple—God's House— and the exile of the Jewish people—God's elected people. In one form or another this problem of theodicy runs right through Jewish history from Abraham's challenge, *Shall not the Judge of all the earth do justly?* (Gen. 18:25), to the agonized questions of the Holocaust generation. In the above story we touch upon a profound idea, that God Himself mourns the destruction and the exile. Now of course, to hold such a belief seems blasphemous, attributing human feelings to God Himself. In principle, a belief which ascribes to God any physical form or emotional experience has no place in the mainstream of classical Jewish teaching. A long time ago Maimonides spoke for a rational Judaism when he insisted that whenever we read in the Bible or in rabbinic literature such anthropomorphisms as the eye of God, His hand, or footstool, or even His anger, sorrow or gladness, they are just figures of speech. God has no human form, nor can we speak of Him as experiencing human emotions such as weeping or mourning for the destruction of the Temple. What then can we learn from Jose's story?

The period of the destruction of the Temple was a watershed age in Jewish history. The Jews had lost their national independence, their land and their freedom. Jews had begun to disperse to every part of the then known world. In retrospect, an objective historian would have been justified in writing that the Jews had reached the end of their national history. But for the rabbis the crisis was not only national or political: it was religious. There was no Temple, no sacrifices, no accepted means of reconciliation or atonement. All the main institutions of organized religion had come down in ruins. At the center of the national agony was the crisis of faith. Could it be that God had rejected Israel? Could it be that God had cancelled His covenant with His people and withdrawn Himself from them?

It is here and in similar stories that rabbinic theology assures the people. The nation's suffering would be hopeless and impossible to bear if the people thought that either God did not know, or did not care. But here the rabbinic story teaches that God knows, God cares and God still loves Israel. The affirmative faith of the poet, "God's in His heaven, all's right with the world!" finds its parallel in the rabbinic legend. God had not deserted Israel. On the contrary, He has compassion for the people in their sorrow, and all will be well in the end. For so long as God knows and "feels" Israel's distress, then the divine covenant with the people remains and the promise of redemption is real.

19

~

The Wandering Jew

Before God commanded Abraham, *Get thee out of thy country, and from thy kindred, and from thy father's house* ... (Gen. 12:1) the patriarch could be likened to a jar of exquisite perfume which was tightly sealed and kept hidden in a remote corner. The superb aroma could not escape and no one could even see it or have any benefit from it. But if the jar were to be uncorked and moved about from room to room then its precious fragrance could be distributed all around. So God said to Abraham, "Abraham, you perform many good deeds and you have taught some of your neighbors the truth about the One God, but the effect is very limited and the world outside knows nothing about you or your faith. Therefore I want you to move about in the world so that your teaching and example can spread and your name will be great in My world, *and I will make of thee a great nation* (Ibid., v. 1). (*S. S. Rab.* 1).

* * *

Jewish history begins with Abraham, the first of the patriarchs. In the Bible, Abraham's story begins with God's summons to leave Ur of the Chaldees. Abraham was seventy-five years old when he received the call, and rabbinic literature fills in more than seven decades of his life with a wealth of folklore, most of it dealing with the patriarch's search for and discovery of the truth about the only One God.

By the time Abraham received the divine call to leave his native country, his teaching of monotheism had made limited impact on his immediate circle. But that was not enough and his influence had to be spread. So the midrashic parable with which we began provides us with the thought that in becoming a wandering Jew Abraham could reach a wider population and thus exercise greater influence.

It is here necessary to point out that in the vast area of rabbinic literature one can find very many different and opposing views. Every time someone tries to prove a point about Judaism by observing that "the Talmud says . . ." what he should really say is "Rabbi X says . . . ." And of course in direct conflict with the opinion of Rabbi X one can find a Rabbi Y who is the author of a contrary statement. This is a leading feature of the free and open discussion and debate which is characteristic of the whole of rabbinic literature. Of course, this in no way implies that rabbinic views are in a chaotic state. Not at all. Whenever it is a question of law, then a decision is taken and the law is finalized and codified. But even in matters of general doctrine there is often a consensus, which in time molds the quality and content of Jewish doctrine and beliefs. The challenge for the student is always to try to discover what is the norm, and the teaching which represents the mainstream in Jewish thought. That, by the way, is what we have attempted in this selection; to discover a story which can be said to illustrate a constant and accepted Jewish theological doctrine.

But sometimes we come across a teaching which is doubtful and we do not know whether it can be described as a constant and accepted Jewish doctrine. In fact, we might find that it goes counter to much in rabbinic theology and might even be rejected by large sections of the Jewish people. The most and the best we can say in such a case is that both contradictory views have a place in the totality of Jewish thought and that normative Judaism is built on the tension of two opposites. Good examples of such opposites in Judaism are universalism and nationalism, Land of Israel centrality and whole world centrality, outward law and inner spirituality. There are times when a pair of opposites seem to be irreconcilable. Nevertheless few will deny the legitimate place of both views within the sum total of Jewish thought. Only time will tell which of the conflicting views becomes representative of the thinking of the mainstream and committed Jewish community.

The present piece is a good example of what we are saying here. The midrash we have quoted is more universalistic and less parochial; it is more pro-dispersion and less Land of Israel centered. It may not represent the view of the majority of the rabbis of the past, and certainly not of the present; but there is absolutely no doubt that it illustrates a school of thought in rabbinic literature. Abraham has to do a little wandering about, to become a "man of the world" in order to influence other peoples. The sweet aroma of the bottle has to be uncorked and moved about so that its benefit can be experienced in other places. The implication is that the dispersion is not such a bad thing; certainly not for the world, and perhaps not even for the Jews. In the same context of ideas we read, "Rabbi Eleazar said: God scattered Israel among the nations for the sole end that proselytes should wax numerous among them. Rabbi Oshaiah said: God did Israel a kindness when He scattered them among the nations" (*Pes.* 87b).

The above view can be seen as an attempt to answer the question of God's justice in permitting the Jews to be exiled from the Promised Land and dispersed throughout the world. Or it might be an attempt on the part of some rabbis to justify themselves in moving to live in the diaspora by giving it a theological legitimacy. In Oshaiah's day the Babylonian Jewish community was growing fast and its importance as the main center of learning was overtaking that of the Holy Land. In later ages—in fact right up to the modern period—such views were quoted to support a historical theory and rationale for the dispersion. It was good for the world. Look at the great contribution which the Jews have made to civilization. Wherever they lived they have enriched society in the fields of philanthropy, science, the arts, scholarship, politics and finance. The Jews can claim a number of Nobel prizes in every field, quite out of proportion to their tiny numbers. The "Wandering Jew" has indeed been a blessing to mankind, fulfilling the prophetic challenge to be a "light unto the nations."

Now of course Zionists argue the case for the modern state of Israel precisely because diaspora Jewish history has been filled with persecution, pogroms, destruction and death. The Holocaust in Nazi Europe was the greatest tragedy for diaspora Jewry, and finally proved that the "dispersion is good" theory is wrong and can even be catastrophic. While the "Wandering Jew" midrash makes certain valid points, particularly the historical truth that the cask of precious perfume which is Abraham and his descendants has been a blessing to mankind, it is also true that the diaspora became the graveyard of untold millions of Abraham's children. The "Wandering Jew" midrash makes its point and some of its implications will always be important, but the Holocaust has virtually invalidated all notions which once attempted to legitimize the dispersal as a blessing.

20

~

Looking to the Future

Moses would not have been born except for the intervention of his sister Miriam. Their father was Amram ben Levi, a leader in the Hebrew community of Egypt. When Pharaoh decreed that every male born among the Hebrews should be destroyed by being thrown into the river to drown (Ex. 1:22) Amram said, "What is the use in having children. They will only be killed by the Egyptian soldiers." So he divorced Jochebed his wife in order to avoid having more children. Because of Amram's status in the Hebrew community, many other husbands followed his example and divorced their wives.

When Miriam realized what had happened she protested to her father. "Your action is worse than Pharaoh's decree" she said. "Pharaoh's decree concerned the fate of the male children only, but your action will prevent the birth of male and female children." She pressed home her argument by adding, "Consider also this, Pharaoh's decree may or may not be carried out. After all, there are babies who will not be found by the Egyptian soldiers and others who will be saved somehow by their parents. Your behavior however will be final and you and mother will have no more children. That much is certain. In addition, see what is happening in our Community. Other men are following your bad example, and if this goes on the future of our people is doomed!"

Amram was persuaded by his daughter's arguments so he went and re-married Jochebed. When the others saw what he had done, they all took back their wives. Some months later Moses was born (*Sot.* 12a; *Sh. Rab.* 1:13).

*   *   *

We may note first of all, that this midrash can be seen as an attempt by the rabbis to explain a text which is rather puzzling. The Bible states, *There went a man of the house of Levi and took to wife a daughter of Levi* (Ex. 2:1). First of all what can we understand by the curious phrase, "and there went a man." Where did he go? Secondly, Amram and Jochebed (the subjects of the sentence and soon to become the parents of the baby Moses) already had two children, Aaron and Miriam, so how can we understand the reference to their marriage in this verse? Surely they were already married and the parents of two children! So our midrash is a classic illustration of rabbinic methods in that they are able to weave a legend which gets around the text and provides an answer to the above two questions. The first on the phrase, "And there went a man," by suggesting that Amram went back to his wife. That is where he went. The second question is answered by the story in a beautiful way. Of course, says the midrash, Amram and Jochebed had been married; and we know that they already had two children. But Amram divorced his wife and then took her back again; and Moses was born.

Now however much the midrash is used for biblical exegesis, it is here suggested that this is not the main purpose of the rabbinic midrash. It is true, of course, that the biblical interpretation is important to the rabbis. But they are much more concerned with the situation of the Jews in their own time, that is, after the destruction of the Temple when the Jews suffered seriously under the oppressive domination of the Romans. Less than fifty years after the destruction, the Romans prohibited the practice of Judaism. Torah study was proscribed on penalty of death, so too the ordination of new rabbis was not permitted. Perhaps worse than anything else, circumcision of newborn male children was strictly prohibited. Under these circumstances, many Jews might have asked, "What is the purpose in having children? We may as well stop marrying, and let the Jews die a natural death!" Indeed there is a statement by the famous Rabbi Ishmael (beginning of second century) who remarked that after the destruction, it could have been decided to stop marriage and the procreation of Jewish children (*B. Bat.* 60b). Our legend treats this same issue by linking the contemporary situation with the suffering of the Hebrew people in Egypt. The Hebrews were trapped in a situation in which there seemed to be no hope at all for the future. Slavery of the most oppressive kind seemed the fate of the Hebrews for all time. And now Pharaoh's decree to kill the male infants seemed to be the final edict which would in time wipe out the tribe altogether. The situation was hopeless and many would have thought that it was meaningless to marry and bring children into a society which would kill them at birth or, at best, enslave them. Such was the thinking of Amram in separating from his wife.

But Miriam seemed to be inspired with greater hope. True, the future was unknown and the worst could happen. But if the Hebrews gave up now and refused to beget children for the future then it would mean that Pharaoh wins in his struggle against the Hebrews. The Hebrews must hope for a better future. More than that: they must do everything possible to assure that there could be a future for the tribe. So she persuades her parents not to give up hope and to live with greater optimism in a coming redemption. In the result, Amram's remarriage to Jochebed resulted in the birth of one who was to become the great leader of the Hebrews who brought them out of Egyptian slavery. When the Bible refers to Miriam as a prophetess (Ex. 15:20), such a designation is charmingly supported by our rabbinic legend.

At the end of the Second World War, after the horrors of the Holocaust were revealed, the thought that it was somehow wrong to beget Jewish children to grow up in a world of murderous Jew-hatred had to be quashed. Instead, it was taught that bringing Jews into a hostile world was an act of faith that must be strengthened. It was not only necessary to replenish Jewish life, but to show the world and the Jews especially that the Jewish people lives on. Hitler could not be given a posthumous victory, and every increase in the Jewish population was an occasion which strengthened the Jewish will and Jewish faith in the future.

In 1939, before the outbreak of the war there were about sixteen million Jews in the world. This number was reduced to ten million during the Holocaust. Almost fifty years later the number of Jews, worldwide, has again risen, to about thirteen million. This in spite of a low Jewish birthrate in the U.S. and in Europe. The most significant fact about Jewish demography today is the encouraging rise of the Jewish population in Israel, which today (1994) is nearly five million. Furthermore about forty-five per cent of Jewish children born all over the world, are today born in Israel. This means that in the foreseeable future most young Jews will be Israeli, and the steady increase in the Jewish population of the Jewish state will more than make up for the decline in the diaspora. The entire subject is an example of the characteristic hopefulness which is an indigenous element in Jewish life and thought. It is no mere coincidence that the Jewish national anthem is titled *Hatikvah*, "the song of hope."

21

~

A Jewish Rip van Winkle

One day Honi Ha-Meagel (the circle drawer) went walking in the hills near Jerusalem when heavy rains began to fall and he was forced to take shelter. He found a secluded cave and went in. Soon he fell into a deep sleep and he remained asleep for seventy years. During that time the First Temple was destroyed by the Babylonians, and the Second Temple was built by those who returned from Babylonian exile more than fifty years later. When Honi woke up he left the cave and saw that everything had changed. Where there had once been vineyards there were now new olive groves, and where there had been olive groves there were now wheat fields. He could not understand what had happened and in his confusion he lost his way into the city and had to ask for directions. When he finally reached Jerusalem he began to ask the people what had been going on to change things so much.

"What's been happening here?" he asked them.

"Why do you ask?" they replied. "Don't you know?"

"No" he answered. "I find everything strange."

"Who are you?" the people wanted to know.

"I am Honi Ha-Meagel" he told them.

The people were not convinced with Honi's story and they refused to believe that he was Honi. But they decided to put his claim to the test. "We have heard that whenever Honi the saint entered the Temple courtyard it immediately lit up." Whereupon Honi made his way to the Temple and as he entered its precincts the whole area was filled with a brilliant light (*J. T.* 3:10).

*   *   *

There are two sages in rabbinic literature with the name of Honi Ha-Meagel. Both were miracle workers and had the reputation of saintliness. Each one got the title "Circle Drawer" from the legend that in a year of severe drought the people came to Honi and pleaded with him to pray for rain. Honi prayed, but without any result. Whereupon Honi drew a circle in the ground, stood in the middle of it, and said, "O Lord of the Universe! Know that I will not move out of this circle until You send rain to relieve the distress of Your people." And the rains came. The more famous of these two lived in the first century B.C.E. The other, perhaps an early ancestor of the latter, lived at the end of the period of the First Temple before it was destroyed by the Babylonians in 586 B.C.E. Both of them were "Rip van Winkle" characters who fell asleep for many years. Our story is about the first Honi.

Before we come to the central question raised by this story, let us see why the author puts Honi to sleep for seventy years. Legends of this kind have parallels in the literature of other people. Essentially, a story-teller uses it as a ploy to transport a character into a period in which he doesn't belong and in that bizarre situation his reactions are the focus of the reader's attention. It is possible that here too an important point of the story is exposed by Honi's reaction to the new world, when, after his initial confusion, he shows his spiritual power by bringing light. Many years ago he brought light. Now too in a strange new world he also brings light. In so doing he shows his authenticity and proves that he is the same Honi.

But now we come to the central question. Why did the rabbis tell this strange story? What lesson did they have for the people? The answer becomes clear when it is realized that the story was written after the destruction of the Second Temple by the Romans in 70 C.E. The historical conditions were generally grim and there was cause for some despair. Roman oppression was driving ever more Jews to leave the country and those who remained were reduced to poverty. Above all there hovered the big theological question, why God allowed the Temple to be destroyed and His people to be slaughtered and persecuted. The rabbinic reaction to this central question finds several different answers in the literature, ranging from one extreme view which openly criticizes God for His silence to the other extreme which accepts the guilt of the Jews as the basic cause for the destruction which is allowed by God as punishment for Israel's sins. Our story represents a very different kind of rabbinic reaction to the national tragedy. The post-Temple period was filled with danger to the very existence of Judaism because without a central shrine, without priests, without sacrifices the people could come to the desperate conclusion that Judaism was finished—at least the Judaism in which they and their ancestors had been nurtured for centuries. The rabbis are intent on showing that a strong Judaism can exist without a Temple. Honi is asleep during the destruction of the First Temple and the erection of the Second Temple. Why? Because the destruction of the one and the building of the other are unimportant. They do not guarantee the preservation of Judaism or prove the authenticity of the Jew. To achieve those goals the Jew has to bring light to the world.

It is as if the rabbis are telling their people who are still agonizing over the destruction of the Temple, "Weep no more! Put aside all your doubts about Judaism without a Temple. We can live without it. The important thing is to live with the light of Torah, with the values of justice, lovingkindness, unity and peace. If we can do that then we prove our identity. Instead of concentrating your attention on buildings of stone look instead to the true source of your spiritual life in obedience to the divine word by which you can bring light to your own lives and illumination to all people who will then recognize the true values of the authentic Jew."

22

~

The Right to the Land

Abraham and his nephew Lot dwelt together in central Canaan when a quarrel broke out between the herdmen of the patriarch and the herdmen of Lot. Both Abraham and his nephew were very rich in cattle, so much so that they had to employ shepherds and herdmen to attend to their cattle. The problem was pasture land. Abraham's herdmen and shepherds kept their master's cattle muzzled when they were on the fields used by Lot's men. But the latter took no notice and thoughtlessly allowed Lot's cattle to roam freely over the fields used by Abraham's servants. This led to a dispute between the herdmen of Abraham and Lot.

"You are robbing our master Abraham of his pasture land" complained Abraham's shepherds.

"Not at all!" retorted Lot's men. "Everyone knows of God's promise to Abraham that the entire land of Canaan will be his. When Abraham dies the land will belong to his descendants. But we all know that Abraham is a barren mule and he will never beget children. The only descendant entitled to the inheritance will be our master Lot, Abraham's nephew. So in fact Lot's cattle are simply pasturing on land that will soon belong to our master!"

God said, "Yes, I have indeed given the land to Abraham and to his descendants, but only after the seven native nations have left the land. However, today the Canaanites and the Perizzites are still living there so they have the right of possession, until the proper time comes for Abraham and his descendants to take it over" (*Ber. Rab.* 41:5).

* * *

The midrashic story relates to the early history of Abraham in Canaan. Basically, the starting point for the legend is the apparent abrupt and unnecessary inclusion in the biblical verse of the reference to the Canaanite and the Perizzites. The full verse is as follows, *And there was a strife between the herdmen of Abram's cattle and the herdmen of Lot's cattle. And the Canaanite and the Perizzite then dwelt in the land* (Gen. 13:7). Now there are several ways open to explain the last part of the verse. The first and most obvious explanation is that there was not enough water for both herds—Abraham's and Lot's—because the land was already inhabited by the native tribes. On another level the abrupt introduction of the Canaanite and the Perizzites into the picture can be given an ethical explanation. Here we have a quarrel between the herdmen of Abraham and Lot: but their masters should have prevented such a quarrel. What sort of example are they showing to the non-believers, i.e., the Canaanites and the Perizzites who were then their neighbors and witnesses to everything that was going on in the Hebrew camp? This could lead to *Hillul Ha-Shem*, bringing disgrace to the Name of God in whom Abraham (and Lot) believed, and shaming their faith. The native tribes could scorn them and say, "What sort of religion is this they believe in, if they cannot live together in peace!" This explanation is reasonable especially in the light of the sequel in which Abraham suggests to Lot that they part and live in different districts, *Let there be no strife, I pray thee, between me and thee, and between my herdmen and thy herdmen; for we are brethren* (Ibid., v. 8).

But our midrash is apparently interested in another approach to the question of the abrupt and perhaps superfluous reference to the Canaanite and Perizzite occupation. God's intervention at the end of the story explains the additional phrase in a rather surprising way. The land was indeed promised to Abraham, but he does not own it yet because the native population is still in the land. Therefore the argument of Lot's herdmen is invalid and they are still guilty of robbery.

As is very common, the authors of the midrash weave their stories and introduce their interpretations of the Bible text with an eye on their contemporary situation. The Romans were in control of Palestine at the time. Undoubtedly they sequestered land which had belonged to Jewish farmers. There must have been occasions when Jewish herdmen let their cattle roam over and pasture in land newly controlled by the Roman occupiers, on the basis of the argument that "The land is ours." Perhaps this midrash is a gentle warning to such people, "Yes the land is yours; but remember the Canaanites and the Perizzites (i.e., the Romans) are now in the land. We will have to wait until the conditions are changed and the Romans are no longer here."

There are very many examples in the Talmud and Midrash where it is clear that the attitude of the rabbis seems to be anti-Roman, militant and activist. Some of the leading rabbis of the period could fit into that class. But then again, we also come across pieces of folklore where the rabbinic attitude is a counsel of patience, of peace and of faith in God's promise of redemption. It is suggested that the above midrash belongs to this group. According to the author, the Jews had suffered more than enough as a result of the Roman wars instigated in large part by fanatical zealots among the Jews. These rabbis would have been adherents of a "peace party" which quietly warned against a repetition of policies which had brought so much suffering to the Jewish people. Theirs was a counsel of accommodation to the contemporary situation in the belief that wise diplomacy rather than military confrontation would gain the Jews relief from oppression.

23

The Valley of Gold

One day Simeon bar Yohai overheard his disciples discussing a fellow student who had left the Holy Land and had gone to another country where he became very rich. The report seemed to excite his students and some of them expressed the desire to follow their colleague's example and seek their own fortune in foreign countries.

On hearing this Simeon became concerned for the future of Torah study in the Land of Israel. So next day he took his students to a spot overlooking a valley in Meron. There he addressed them, "If it is money you want, here it is. Take as much as you wish." So saying, he called on the valley to fill up with gold, and golden coins began to pour down. "But you should be warned" added the rabbi "that whoever picks up the gold will be reducing his share in the World to Come where the ultimate reward awaits every sincere student of Torah" (*Sh. Rab.* 52:3).

* * *

It would be nice to assume that the students took the lesson to heart and returned to the study house with their master. But we don't know the end of the story. At all events we have to investigate the lesson it teaches.

Rabbi Simeon bar Yohai is a famous and legendary figure in rabbinic literature. He lived in the middle of the second century and survived the grim years of the post-Bar Kokhba period when Roman rule in Palestine was especially oppressive. Simeon was an outspoken Jewish nationalist, and on one occasion he brought on himself the sentence of death for criticizing the harsh domination of the military rulers. He fled, and the legend has it that he hid in a cave for several years.

On coming out of hiding he lived in Meron in the Galilee and there he continued to teach Torah with his unique emphasis on the concepts of Jewish freedom including love for the Land of Israel.

Judaism knows of several great loves, in addition to the experience of human love. There is love of God which is the supreme love. Then there is love of the Torah, and love of the Land of Israel. Our story illustrates this last love, which in Jewish thought is raised to a theological concept of some significance.

The relationship of the people and the land is persistent right from the beginning of Jewish history. The Bible antedates that relationship even before there is a Hebrew tribe. God made a covenant with Abraham, and the first divine word addressed to the patriarch was, *Get out of your land . . . and up to the land which I will show you* (Gen. 12:1). God promised the patriarchs Abraham, Isaac and Jacob that their descendants would possess the Land of Canaan. There was yet no Jewish people, but their future title to the land was already declared.

This bond of the people to the Promised Land was not upset either by later enemy invasions of the country or by the dispersal of the Jews all over the world. Those sad events were interpreted as part of the biblical prophecy concerning the destruction of the land because of the sins of the people. Yet in spite of all this, God would finally remember His covenant with Abraham, with Isaac and with Jacob, *and I will remember the land* (Lev. 26:42). The promise was that Israel and the land will be redeemed, and the people will return to its former borders.

This mystic embrace of people and land is closely connected to the belief in Israel as the chosen people. Whatever interpretation we give to this concept, it means, at the least, that the Jewish people is different from other people in its religion and in its history, from which it evolved a set of unique ideals and responses to historical challenge. This uniqueness was related to the ideal of developing the highest ethical conduct of man in society, and to reaching the maximum spiritual potential of the individual.

To achieve this, Jews and Judaism had to have a geographic base. So the land became important, since without it there could have been no people and without the people there would have been no Judaism.

This idea impressed itself so markedly into the life and thought of the Jews that it entered into the legislation of the law makers. They ruled, for example, that if a slave wished to go to the Holy Land, his master must either follow him or free him. Conversely, if the master wishes to leave Eretz Israel his slave need not follow him. In another ruling, refusal on the part of a spouse to settle in the Holy Land is a valid cause for divorce.

In our own time, settlement in Eretz Israel has again been stressed as one of the great values in Jewish life, because the Land of Israel has again become the heart of a living Jewish people returning to its source, and expressing through its reattachment to the land its will to reenter history. For centuries, Israel's dedication to the biblical covenant which united it with the land was kept alive through prayer and hope. Now the period of waiting is over, and the land is seen again as a tangible and central element in the will of the people to live with the reality and challenge of the biblical title to the land.

All that is theology, and a description of the ideal. But the reality is often a cruel antagonist militating against living with the ideal. Thus, under Roman rule and especially in the Hadrianic period, conditions in the Holy Land were very difficult indeed. Roman oppression was severe; for a time the practice of Judaism was prohibited on penalty of death; the land became impoverished and Jews were leaving the country to find their livelihood in foreign lands. This was the situation at the time of Rabbi Simeon bar Yohai. Even then they had the problem, painfully modern, of *yeridah*—emigration from the Holy Land. As Rabbi Simeon saw it, the intentions of his students were particularly reprehensible since they could endanger the whole future of Torah study in Eretz Israel.

There is no way of explaining how the valley could fill up with gold coins. Perhaps the rabbi assembled them at sunset, and as the glow of the setting sun fell on the stones, the golden sheen provided the rabbi with a visible symbol to drive home his message—which was that by living and studying Torah in the Holy Land they have a spiritual treasure which is more valuable than all the gold they could imagine.

ETHICS

24

~

Sanctifying God's Name

One day Simeon ben Shetah asked his servant to go to the market and buy him a donkey. The servant did as he was asked and soon came back with a donkey which he bought from its Arab owner. Then when the rabbi's disciples came to examine the ass they found a precious jewel suspended from the animal's neck. They ran to congratulate their master on his good fortune and cried out, "Praised be God who has sent you this great fortune!" But Simeon thought otherwise about the unexpected find. "I bought only the ass, and not this precious stone" he said, and he himself went back to the Arab to make certain that the jewel was returned to its owner. When the Arab realized what Simeon had done for him he was overcome with admiration for the Jewish teacher and exclaimed, "Praised be the God of Simeon ben Shetah!" (*Dev. Rab.* 3:3).

*   *   *

Rabbi Simeon ben Shetah was one of the most interesting and important rabbinic personalities in the early rabbinic era. He lived in the first century B.C.E. He was a leader of the Pharisees who established the rabbinic interpretation of Scriptures which laid the basis for the codification of the law, and which became the authentic expression of normative Judaism. His sister was Queen Salome Alexandra; but his relationship to his brother-in-law King Alexander Jannai was less than cordial. In fact, for many years he was persecuted by the king

because the rabbi's Pharisaic policy went counter to the king's Sad-
ducean sympathies.

Numerous stories are told about Simeon, anecdotes about his
public career, his life as a member of the queen's family, and of his
major role as a religious leader. The above story tells of an incident in
his private life, and unlike most of the others in this collection it is
probably historical rather than purely folkloristic.

The story is a classic piece, often told to illustrate the central
Jewish ethic of *Kiddush Ha-Shem*—the sanctification of God's Name.
That Hebrew value term is often associated with martyrdom. Thus,
countless heroes who have been killed because of their loyalty to
God and Judaism are said to have died for *Kiddush Ha-Shem*. But it
is often forgotten that one can also live for *Kiddush Ha-Shem*.
Whenever a Jew lives a life of absolute integrity with standards
which are unambiguously ethical then he is said to live a life of *Kiddush Ha-Shem*, sanctifying the Name of God, because he brings
honor to Judaism and the Jew.

The Arab merchant knew that Simeon ben Shetah was a Jew who
worshiped God, and when he realized that Simeon's honesty was motivated by his religious ethic then he praised the God worshiped by
Simeon. In quite a literal sense then Simeon's honest deed was an act
of *Kiddush Ha-Shem* which evoked from the Arab a recognition of
God and a blessing of His Name.

In a general sense everything which a Jew might do which up-
holds the name of Jew and Judaism is an act of *Kiddush Ha-Shem*.
This is the highest religious value to which a Jew can aspire; just as
the reverse, the negative *Hillul Ha-Shem*—the profanation of God's
Name—is the most heinous offence of which a Jew can be guilty.

It is important to note that the value of *Kiddush Ha-Shem* as well
as its opposite are generally related to man's social behavior. The admiration and the blessing of the Arab resulted not really from the rabbi's religious piety but from his honesty to his fellow man. And this
leads us to an important consideration.

Sometimes one learns of a Jew with a reputation of being religious who commits a social offence against the moral or state laws. In
such a situation the question is asked how a religious Jew can be
guilty of unethical behavior. The plain answer is that such a person
is not religious. He may be careful in his observance of the ritual law,
even to the extent of being punctilious about the smallest detail but
if his behavior is unethical, say in his business or in his domestic life,
then such a person cannot be called religious. He is a ritualist: and
no more than that. And ritualism, though it is important in a life of

personal piety, is valid only when it is a part of the organic whole of Jewish teaching.

It is an old discussion this, the comparative importance of ritual and ethics. As far as Judaism is concerned the question is really invalid because both sides of Judaism are important. A man whose life is completely ethical but who keeps nothing of the religious culture or the ritual of Judaism does not merit the honorable title, "a good Jew." He may be correctly described as "a good man," but then members of other religious groups and even agnostics and atheists are frequently "good men." In the context of our present discussion however, the term "a good Jew" is more comprehensive and will certainly embrace loyalty to the specific Jewish religious laws and culture as part of the lifestyle of the Jew.

On the other hand—and it is impossible to exaggerate this point—a person who is a zealot for the ritual law but is guilty of un-ethical behavior is a "religious" cripple who hobbles along on only one leg of Judaism, and even that leg is seriously diseased; because where morality is absent the rest is hypocrisy and humbug. Ritual cannot be the single dimension of the religious life. Where the ethical non-ritualist at least earns the description of being a good man the im-moral ritualist is nothing; neither a good Jew nor a good man.

That is why the lovely story of Simeon ben Shetah and his honest act of *Kiddush Ha-Shem* is frequently quoted in our literature as an il-lustration and reminder of the centrality of ethics in Jewish teaching.

25

Alexander and the Skull

One day when the Greek king and conqueror Alexander the Great was returning from his triumphant marches through Africa, he rested by a peaceful lake for some refreshment. He was given some salty fish which he washed in the water of the lake, and as a result the fish had a most wonderful taste. He then bathed his face in the water which he found extraordinarily pure, refreshing and fragrant. "This lake has its source in the garden of Eden" he said. So he traced its source through much winding territory until he finally came to Eden. "Let me in!" he called out. But the guardians of Paradise refuse him entry. "Then give me some memento to show that I've been here" he requested. And they gave him a small piece of a human skull. "Here you are" they said. "Take this home with you and learn from it what you can."

When the great king returned home he placed the bone on one side of the scales and some gold on the other side, but the tiny bone outweighed the gold. The powerful conqueror then heaped more and more gold on the scales, but however much gold he added, it made absolutely no difference: the tiny bone weighed down all the precious metal. Finally, he called together all his wise counsellors and asked them to explain the strange phenomenon. The sages took the bone and examined it very carefully. Then they came back to the king and said, "Sire, the bone you gave us to examine is part of a human skull around the eye socket. The reason it outweighs all the gold is because the eye of man is never satisfied. However much gold and other treasures are heaped up, the eye still wants more."

"Is there any way in which the true weight of this little bone can be seen?" the king asked. "Yes, there certainly is" they answered. So saying, the chief of the wise men took a handful of earth and sprinkled some of it on the bone. Immediately, the scale holding it jumped right up and the heavy gold on the other side went down. "See" he said to the king, "all we had to do was to put a little earth on the eye socket. For this is the end to all man's acquisitions of wealth and ambition for power. When the earth covers him he reaches that point in every man's destiny when his possessions are left behind, when gold is of no more avail to him, and when his true and ultimate value is seen in all its clarity" (*Tam.* 32b).

* * *

In general, the rabbinic literature deals kindly with Alexander the Great, and it is of passing interest to see in this tale that the world conqueror tastes a little of the fragrance of Paradise and actually arrives at the gates of Eden. There are several other rabbinic folk tales which portray Alexander in a sympathetic light, and all this may be a recognition of his place as a somewhat benevolent ruler of the Jews and the Holy Land.

But to return to our story. The lesson is clear, and it is basically a homily on the futility of man's quest for material wealth. At times man is greedy, and the more he sees the more he wants. His greed is such that it can become his dominant emotion so that there is no end to his struggle for greater acquisitions. The end of his quest for material things then comes with death itself—when the eye is covered over with the dust of the earth.

Now this kind of lesson is not unusual and the moral of the story is illustrated by many ethical teachings of the same genre which are found all over rabbinic literature. A similar ethical teaching is seen in the popular saying of the second-century Ben Zoma who taught, "Who is rich? He who is satisfied with what he has" (*Avot* 4:1).

This being the case, it is not out of place to point out that in Jewish ethics material possessions as such are not in themselves evil. There is nothing at all wrong in a man wanting to be rich, or in being rich. Perhaps in this respect Judaism is rather unique in its healthy acceptance of the legitimate pursuit of material prosperity and happiness. In fact the prayer for a new month includes a petition for material sufficiency side by side with the prayer for spiritual and religious fulfillment. God made everything good to be enjoyed, and Judaism has been called "the cheery creed" because it gladly embraces the world of the senses and all legitimate enjoyments which it can provide. Where other religious disciplines will raise asceticism and celibacy to an ideal, Judaism regards such extreme abstention from the enjoyment of the gifts of the physical world as a sin. Even the nazirite who only abstained from wine was required to bring a sin offering at the conclusion of his period of abstention. On the other hand Judaism does not elevate the material world to a position of priority in human values. If sex, wealth, food and all the other material and sensual pleasures of life are not sins, neither are they sacred. They are placed in the category of the neutral with the potential of becoming one thing or the other—sin or holy. It all depends on their use. Thus sex is sanctified by the laws of Jewish marriage, food becomes an element in the total religious experience through the observance of the dietary code, and material possessions become a great human value if they are acquired ethically and are used with charity. If wealth is sought in moderation and used with benevolence, then possessions can be a source of great blessing. In a few words, the quest for wealth is not an evil. Only the unrestrained pursuit of wealth is evil because then the man can become totally obsessed by his possessions.

The moral of our story then is a homily only against an unsatiable yearning for wealth where no amount of gold seems to satisfy and where man is driven throughout his life by an all powerful urge to heap up more and ever more possessions. If that happens, then the man has to be reminded that his end is the dust and that when his life is over then all his worldly goods leave him and are worthless to him.

26

~

Selfless Love

One of the worst kinds of infectious disease known in the Talmud was *raathan*. It is described as a disease of the skin which causes extreme debility and is highly contagious. The scholars give some stern warnings against even indirect contact with a diseased person because such contact was considered fatal.

However, it is told about the third century sage and mystic, Rabbi Joshua ben Levi, that he would sit with an unfortunate sufferer of *raathan*, and even study with him, hoping that the Torah would guard them both. It was an act of total love of fellow man, even to the point of endangering his own life.

The Talmud does not tell us if the rabbi succumbed to the dread disease, but relates the following story of his last moments.

When the time came for Rabbi Joshua ben Levi to die, the Angel of Death was instructed to present himself to the rabbi and help him in any matter which he requested. When the angel appeared, the rabbi asked, "Will you show me my place in the next world?" Death answered, "Yes. Come with me and I will show you."

"But I want you first to hand over your sword" said Joshua, "because you might scare me on the way." So the angel handed over his weapon and off they went.

They soon reached Paradise, where Joshua was shown his place of honor. When he saw it, the rabbi quickly jumped over the fence which separated both worlds and he landed on the side of Paradise. But the angel just managed to hold on to the rabbi's coat and prevented him from disappearing altogether.

"Give me back my sword!" demanded Death.

"No" said the rabbi. "I will not come back and I will not return your sword."

At this, a heavenly voice ordered Rabbi Joshua to give back the sword to the Angel of Death. "It is his tool and he needs it to carry out the divine plan and to cut the thread of life." So the rabbi returned the weapon and was then escorted to his place in Paradise.

Now, Rabbi Joshua had a dear colleague and friend named Hanina ben Pappa, who tried to do the same thing. When his time came to die, the Angel of Death was instructed to present himself to the rabbi, and when Death came to Hanina, the rabbi requested a reprieve.

"Give me thirty days to review my Torah knowledge, then I will be better prepared to enter into the world of total truth" he said. The angel granted his request and, when he came back to claim the rabbi's soul, Hanina asked, "Can I see my place in the World to Come?"

"Yes, of course" answered Death. "Just follow me."

"But first give me your sword in case you frighten me on the way" said the rabbi. But the angel refused.

"Why not?" persisted Hanina. "You bring me a copy of the Torah and you will see that there is nothing which I have transgressed or failed to do! You let Rabbi Joshua have your sword. Is my knowledge of Torah any less than his?"

The Angel of Death replied, "You cannot compare yourself to Rabbi Joshua ben Levi. Did you ever sit and study with a man suffering with the *raathan* disease?" (*Ket.* 77b).

*   *   *

There are two separate lessons in this folklore. The first is that the Angel of Death cannot be disarmed. No one can take his sword or obstruct him from carrying out his allotted task. Death is the final destiny of every man. It is a natural part of life itself and, in fact, is the only certainty in the whole of life. Rabbi Joshua had to learn that lesson when he was ordered to return the sword to the Angel of Death.

The second lesson is a teaching about love and its supremacy in the hierarchy of human values. Joshua's compassion for the suffering victim of *raathan* was so great that it outweighed every other human quality.

When Hanina tried to do the same as Joshua and get the angel's sword, he claimed his study and his knowledge of Torah as his great achievement. The thirty days reprieve to review his learning was a recognition of his dedication to Torah.

But at the end, the angel challenges him, "How can you compare yourself to Joshua? You never sat with a sufferer of *raathan*!" So all Hanina's knowledge and piety, while they were great and important, were not as precious as Joshua's selfless acts of altruistic love for a suffering fellow.

This lesson is significant. It is often said that Judaism lays less emphasis on love of one's fellow man than on the social values of justice, or the value of Torah study. But such a view is far from the truth.

Certainly, Judaism emphasizes the importance of justice, truth, peace and other values as the foundations of an ordered society. It also recognizes the centrality of Torah study as a supporting pillar of Jewish life. But it is highly doubtful if they would be regarded in the mainstream of Jewish ethics as higher than the value of love.

For an ordered society the social values are supreme, and Torah study is basic to the preservation of Judaism and the Jewish people. But for a life of piety and inner spirituality, Judaism would emphasize the first quality of love.

Thou shalt love thy neighbour as thyself (Lev. 19:18) was taught by Akiba as the highest ethic of Judaism. And before him the famous Hillel the Elder taught a similar ethic. Of course it is true that the rabbis also generally recognized that there was a problem how to draw a line between love of fellow man and self-sacrifice, and they did not believe that a man is called upon to perform an act of self-sacrifice in pursuing the ethic of love of fellow man.

Nevertheless, there is still room in Judaism for the ideal of selfless love which seems to have no limits. This is the lesson illustrated in our story.

27

~

Kindness to Animals

One day Rabbi Judah the Prince was walking to the study house when he saw a farmer leading a calf to be slaughtered. As the great rabbi passed, the calf ran to the rabbi and hid under his long coat for protection. The animal seemed to be pleading with the rabbi to be saved from its death. Whereupon Rabbi Judah sent the animal back to its owner. "Go!" he said "since this is what you were created for." Immediately it was decreed in heaven, "Because Judah showed no compassion to the dumb animal therefore let him be afflicted with painful illness." Thereafter the rabbi suffered from agonising illness for several years.

Then one day while Rabbi Judah's servant maid was cleaning the house she came upon some tiny mice which she began to sweep away into the yard. The rabbi happened to notice what she was doing and he said to her, "Leave them alone, for our Bible teaches that *His tender mercies are over all His works* (Ps. 145:9)." After that, a new heavenly decree announced, "Because Rabbi Judah showed compassion let his pains leave him." And the rabbi was cured (*Bab. Metz.* 85a).

*   *   *

Rabbi Judah was titled the "Prince" which is the literal translation of his Hebrew designation—*nasi*, a title given to leaders of the rabbinic Sanhedrin of sages and elders who were the highest authority in the Jewish Community of Palestine. The first *nasi* was the famous Hillel of the first century, and all subsequent "princes" were direct descendants of Hillel. With the exception of the period of severe persecution at the time of the Hadrianic oppression when there was no *nasi*, the patriarchal name remained continuous until 425 C.E. with the death of Gamaliel IV.

Judah lived at the end of the second and the first part of the third centuries and was the sixth in the line of succession from Hillel. He was a man of great wisdom, scholarship, wealth and influence and one of the greatest rabbinic leaders of all time. But his chief claim to fame was his work as the compiler and editor of the six orders of the Mishnah, the entire body of Jewish oral law, as it had developed over the centuries up until his day.

The above anecdote is literally one of scores of stories told about Rabbi Judah the Prince. Its moral is clearly the ethic of kindness to animals. This value is known by its Hebrew term, *Tzaar Baalei Hayyim*, literally, the law against causing "pain to any living creature."

The text which Rabbi Judah quotes from one of the most popular of all the psalms has the Hebrew *Ve-rahamav al kol ma'asav*. The key word here is *rahamim*, usually translated "compassion." It is an interesting word which derives from the root *rehem*, meaning a "womb," connoting a number of ideas including compassion as a root feeling of life, and compassion as profound as a woman's feelings for the child born from her own womb. A modern Jewish thinker taught that compassion is the central value of Judaism and that a person without compassion cannot live as a Jew. Moreover, compassion is to be extended not only to all humans but also to animals. This is not an ethic which one would have expected in the Middle East, yet it is found stressed again and again in our sources beginning with the Bible. Here are just a few of the more prominent texts:

If thou see the ass of him that hateth thee lying under its burden, thou shalt forbear to pass by him; thou shalt surely release it with him (Ex. 23:5). The fact that the owner of the poor beast is an enemy does not enter into the situation in which the animal has fallen under its load.

If a bird's nest chance to be before thee in the way, in any tree or on the ground, with young ones or eggs and the dam sitting upon the young, or upon the eggs, thou shalt not take the dam with the young; thou shalt in any wise let the dam go, but the young thou mayest take unto thyself; that it may be well with thee, and that thou mayest prolong thy days (Deut. 22:6, 7). Here the Bible teaches that one should be sensitive even to the feelings of the mother bird. As if to say, it is bad enough that you are taking away the eggs or the young; but don't do it in the presence of the mother bird in order to avoid inflicting additional pain.

Thou shalt not plough with an ox and an ass together (Ibid. 22:10). The reason is that they are animals of different strength and the powerful ox would naturally drag the weak ass along with it, causing discomfort and pain to the weaker animal.

Thou shalt not muzzle the ox when he treadeth out the corn (Ibid. 25:4). When the threshing animal is working in the corn field it would be the height of cruel insensitivity to prevent the working beast from eating as it moves along the grain.

Finally, the rabbis who showed great feeling for this ethic taught that one should not sit down to eat before seeing that his animals have been fed. They even found a biblical support for their teaching by quoting the verse from the second paragraph of the Shema, *And I will give grass in thy fields for thy cattle, and thou shalt eat and be satisfied* (Ibid. 11:15). Here the Bible clearly indicates food for the cattle before sustenance for its owner.

It is told of the Hassidic master David of Lelov (Poland, eighteenth century), that he would be missing from the prayer house while the shofar was being blown during the month of Elul. His followers found him feeding his horse. He must have thought that kindness to animals is more important even than listening to the shofar.

28

The Quality of Patience

One day two men had a wager about the extraordinary forbearance of the great sage Hillel. One of them said that in spite of all the stories about the rabbi he could make Hillel angry, and the other bet him four hundred zuzim that he would fail.

The first man accepted the wager and worked out his plan. Next Friday, a few hours before the onset of the Sabbath, when he knew that the great Hillel was preparing for the holy day, he went to the rabbi's house just when Hillel was bathing, pounded on the door and yelled "Where is Hillel! Where is Hillel!" The rabbi put on his robe and went out to greet the crude intruder.

"What can I do for you, my son?" Hillel asked.

"I have an important question for you" answered the man.

"Tell me what it is you wish to know" said the rabbi.

"I want to know why Babylonians have such round heads."

"That is a very good question" said Hillel. "I believe it is because the midwives in Babylon are not so skilled."

The man went away and waited for a while until Hillel resumed his personal preparation for the Sabbath. Then he went back to the house, again banged at the door and yelled at the top of his voice, "Where is Hillel! Where is Hillel!"

Once again, the rabbi dressed and went down to see the man and asked "What can I do for you, my son?"

"I want to ask you another important question" said the man.

"Very well, then," said the gentle sage, "what is your question?"

"I want to know why the Tadmoreans have such weak eyes" he said.

"That is also a good question" answered Hillel. "It is because they live in a very sandy country and the wind often blows sand in their eyes."

The man left for a second time, but came back again as soon as he thought Hillel would have resumed his ablutions for the Sabbath. Once more he banged at the door and rudely yelled out for Hillel. And for the third time Hillel went out to him and asked, "What is it you want, my child?"

"I have another question for you" said the man. "Why do the Africans have such broad feet?"

"Another good question" said Hillel. "It is because they live in very marshy land and they need broad feet to get along."

The man then said, "I have many more questions to ask, but I am afraid I might make you angry."

At this, Hillel wrapped his robe more tightly around himself, sat down on the ground in front of the man and said, "You may ask all the questions you want to."

"Are you the Hillel whom people call the leader in Israel?"

"I believe I am" said the rabbi.

"Then I hope that there are not many more like you!"

"Why do you say that?" asked the astonished Hillel.

"Since I lost four hundred zuzim because of you," said the man, and he told him the story of his wager.

"Well" said Hillel, "it is better that you should lose such bets again and again rather than that Hillel should lose his temper."

A Gentile once asked Shammai, "How many kinds of Torah do you Jews have?" Shammai answered, "We have two Torahs, one is the Written Law and the other is the Oral Law." The Gentile then said, "I am ready to accept the Written Law but not the Oral Law, and I ask you to convert me to Judaism on my commitment only to the Written Law." Shammai unceremoniously dismissed him from his house.

The Gentile then went to Hillel with the same question and the same request. Hillel agree to convert him and he began to teach him the aleph bet. On the next day Hillel continued to teach him but gave the letters different names. "Yesterday" said the man "you taught me that these letters had different names." Hillel answered him, "So you see that you have to rely on my oral teaching to explain the written letters. In the same way the Written Law depends for its interpretation on the Oral Law. The Gentile accepted the explanation, continued to study and became a convert to Judaism.

Another Gentile once came to Shammai and said, "I want you to teach me the whole of Judaism in a nutshell and then convert me." Shammai chased him out of his house, and the man then went to Hillel with the same request. Hillel agreed and said, "The essence of Judaism can be summed up in the teaching, 'Do not unto others what you would not like them to do to you.' The rest of the Torah is the commentary, which you should now study." That man also became a convert to Judaism.

On another occasion a Gentile passed the study hall of the rabbis when he heard a sage expounding the verse, *And these are the garments which they shall make: a breast plate, and an ephod* . . . (Ex. 28:4). "For whom are these garments made?" he asked. "For the high priest" he was told. Then he thought, 'I could become a high priest.' And he went to Shammai and said, "Convert me to Judaism so that I can be appointed high priest." Shammai had a building rod in his hand and he chased the man away. But the Gentile then went to Hillel. "Convert me" he said "and then make me high priest." Hillel agreed, but said to the man, "You agree of course that a man cannot become king until he first of all learns the ways and protocols of royalty; so now you should go and study the laws relating to the priesthood." The man went to learn, and when he came across the law, that the stranger who touches the sacred items of the tabernacle is put to death (Num. 1:51), he asked, "To whom does that refer?" He was told, "Even to King David himself." When he heard that, he applied the law to his own case. "If an Israelite, one of the people called 'children of God' and one whom God calls 'My son,' 'My firstborn' can incur the penalty of death if he should unlawfully touch the sacred things in the tabernacle, how much more so for a simple proselyte like me who was not even born a Jew!"

One day those three men who had become proselytes happened to meet and they agreed, "The quick temper of Shammai could have chased us away from the true life. But the gentleness and patience of Hillel brought us under the wings of the Divine Presence' (*Shab.* 30b).

*   *   *

The moral of all the above stories is pretty much the same, and it is the ethic of patience. In the first story the man who tried to make Hillel angry tried his very best. He chose the worst time for Hillel, the eve of Sabbath, when he knew that the sage would be preparing for the holy day. Further his manner was offensively rude, banging at

the rabbi's door and yelling for him. Third his questions were absolutely ridiculous. More than that, the first one was insulting since Hillel himself was a Babylonian. Yet in spite of all this provocation, not
only does Hillel not lose his temper, but his attitude to the man is
positively courteous.

The other stories about Gentiles who wished to convert, while
they also emphasize the quality of Hillel's extraordinary patience,
raise one or two additional matters. The first is related to Hillel's remarkable teaching method. One can teach only with love, and teaching with love Hillel succeeded where Shammai failed. The other
point of interest is the procedure Hillel adopted in handling potential
converts to Judaism. His method was motivated by his desire to bring
all people closer to God, Torah and Judaism. In all three cases Shammai's responses illustrate the harsh and demanding policy which
achieved nothing at all. This was the attitude reflected in an initial re-
quirement that all requests for conversion be accompanied by a commitment to accept every law and observance, even the smallest;
otherwise the request was immediately rejected. The other policy is
that of Hillel as illustrated in our stories. It is a policy of human kindness, of understanding and sympathy, and especially a policy of gradu-
alism—that is one which accepts that the convert cannot embrace
every law of Judaism right from the beginning. His change may be
gradual, and his introduction to Judaism will be measured in a step by
step progress into his new life.

The nice little epilogue in which the three converts exchange
their views on Shammai's failure and Hillel's success underlines the
validity of the above interpretation.

29

~

Above Suspicion

In the final decades of the Second Temple there were two famous families, the family of Garmu and the family of Abtinos, whose fame arose from a rather unique skill. The Garmu family were the experts in baking the showbread for the Temple. Twelve special loaves were placed on the golden table of the Sanctuary and exchanged for new ones each week. The Abtinos family were the experts in making the incense used in the Temple ritual by the priests.

The elders of the Garmu family decided not to teach their skills to anyone outside the family, and the same decision was made by the Abtinos elders. The result was that the special method of baking the showbread for the Temple and the holy incense was a closely guarded secret which no one outside those two families could ever learn.

Now the rabbis were not happy with the policy of the families and were afraid that the Temple service would be endangered if they allowed such a monopoly to continue. So they called in other specialist bakers and perfumery experts from Alexandria in Egypt to replace the two families. But things did not go at all well. The new bakers were unable to make the Temple loaves last fresh all week, like the showbread of Garmu; and the incense of the Alexandrians did not send its smoke up in a perfectly straight line like the Abtinos incense.

So the Temple heads called in the heads of the two old families, but they refused to come. Finally, after their fee was doubled, they came before the Temple administrators who asked them why they do not instruct others in their skills. The Garmu and Abtinos patriarchs gave the same answer. They said, "We know that our holy Temple will be destroyed and we are afraid that if outsiders know how we make the showbread and the incense for the Temple then some of them might go along and make them for purposes of idolatry. The Temple leaders were satisfied with the explanation, and to the very end the method of making the showbread and the incense remained a closely guarded secret.

In addition to their passionate concern that items used in the holy Temple would not be misused for idolatrous or secular purposes, the families of Garmu and Abtinos were highly praised for their moral concern that no one in their families should be suspected of using Temple material for their own purposes. That is why members of the Garmu family never ate pure bread loaves in case anyone would suspect them of eating Temple loaves or using the baking material for their own use. Similarly the women members of the Abtinos family never wore perfume so that there would never be any suspicion that they were taking some Temple incense ingredients for their private use. Indeed, they were so firm in this matter that before one of their men married a lady from another family, they stipulated to the bride that perfume was not to be used by their womenfolk, in order to rise above suspicion (*Yoma* 38a).

*   *   *

These anecdotes about the families Garmu and Abtinos seem to have some basis in history, but here we shall concentrate only on the ethical lesson which is illustrated, and specifically just one ethical lesson which we derive from the latter part of the *aggadah*.

The members of the two families avoided eating fine bread and wearing perfume for the simple and clear reason that they wished to avoid all suspicion that they had misappropriated Temple materials. But the question could be asked, 'Why should they concern themselves to satisfy public opinion, so long as they themselves knew that they were innocent of such misdemeanors? Was it fair to require them to be looking behind their backs all the time wondering, What will the neighbors think?' Of course, strictly speaking, it wasn't fair, and so long as they knew that they were absolutely innocent they could have been left alone to eat their own bread, whatever it was, and for their women to wear their perfume, so long as it was totally their own property.

But there is a nice ethic in the story. That is the ethic known in Hebrew as *Marit Ayin*, loosely translated as "For the sake of appearance." That is, a situation should not only be correct, but it should appear to others that it is correct. In that way, observers will derive a good example from witnessing what is right, and they will be protected from a bad example if they see something that appears to be wrong. A great judge once declared that it is not only necessary that justice be done; it is important that justice be seen to be done. That will give the people greater confidence in the rightness of the law and in the fairness of its administration. And a similar idea can be applied to other values. In Orthodox Jewish circles an observant Jew may be taught not to go window-shopping on the Sabbath. Although he knows that he is not going to desecrate the holy day by going in to buy, yet there could be a danger that someone who does not know him may pass and see him examining the goods in the window with the intention of doing some shopping, and that would lead to a weakening of the Sabbath in the eyes of the stranger.

The ethic has wider implications in the behavior of a community leader whose actions have to be free from all suspicion. After the children of Israel had completed the construction of the tabernacle in the wilderness, the Bible records that Moses made a complete record of how every item had been used, the gold and the silver, the brass and every precious item was accounted for, to the very last piece. Why did he do this? Surely the great prophet of God could be trusted to execute his mission with perfect honesty! The rabbinic *aggadah* however suggests the answer along the lines we have already indicated. It was not only necessary for Moses to be innocent in the sight of God; it was also important for him to be innocent in the eyes of the people. More than anything else, a leader has to be completely above suspicion.

In making the agreement with the tribes of Reuben and Gad, Moses allows them to settle east of the Jordan on condition that first of all their men cross over to the west in order to help the other tribes conquer the territory. Then, and only then, could they take possession of the region on the east side. If they will do that, says Moses, then they will be innocent in the eyes of God and in the eyes of the people (Num. 32:22). The extra phrase is highly significant. Again, it is not only necessary to be innocent in God's sight; it is also vital to be guiltless in the informed opinion of the people. The Bible records of the boy Samuel, *And the child Samuel grew on, and increased in favour both with the Lord, and also with men* (1 Sam. 2:26). The Book of Proverbs contains the beautiful instruction of the writer to his son about the importance he should attach to the values of kindness and truth. If the young man keeps close to them in his daily life then he has the key by which he will *find grace and good favour in the sight of God and man* (Prov. 3:4). In these and other texts the connection is made between the "opinion" of God and the opinion of ones fellow man. Ultimately they are joined. The famous first century teacher Hanina ben Dosa taught this when he said to his disciples, "He in whom the spirit of his fellow men is pleased, in him the Spirit of God is pleased; and he in whom the spirit of his fellow men is not pleased, in him the Spirit of God is not pleased" (*Avot*, 3:13).

30

The Penitent King

Manasseh was one of the last rulers of the kingdom of Judah. His father, Hezekiah, was an upright and God-fearing man whose righteous reign is praised in the Bible. But his son, Manasseh, was quite the opposite, and during his long reign of fifty-five years he re-introduced idol worshipping cults throughout the land. But there was even worse.

Rabbi Simeon ben Azzai told that he found in Jerusalem an old genealogical and historical record in which was written "Manasseh murdered Isaiah." What happened was as follows. When the king set up an idol in the Temple, Isaiah the prophet, who was in fact Manasseh's grandfather, confronted the king and his followers. In daring words he rebuked them in the name of God and said, "Why do you boast about this Temple? The whole universe is not big enough to contain God, and you are stupid if you think you can find His Presence here, especially as you have so flagrantly defiled it with all your abominations. In any event, the king of Babylon will destroy it; the land will be conquered and you will be taken captives and exiled."

Manasseh was furious. "Arrest him!" he ordered his soldiers. Isaiah managed to escape and ran to a forest where he hid in the hollow of a cedar, which miraculously closed up to conceal the prophet. But the fringes of his garment were visible on the outside of the tree. The soldiers returned to the palace and reported to the king where Isaiah was hiding, whereupon the king ordered his woodsmen to cut the tree in two. They did so, and as they were carrying out the king's cruel order, Isaiah died an appalling death as his blood seeped through the tree.

Some time later, Manasseh tried to break Assyria's domination over Judah; but he was unsuccessful, and as a result of his abortive revolt the Assyrians imprisoned and cruelly tortured him causing him great suffering. The Assyrians had a particularly grim torture machine in which their victims were virtually roasted alive. They put Manasseh inside this machine and began to heat the coals. When the Judean king saw the terrible fate that was upon him he began to call on every idol he knew pleading for its help. One god after another was invoked, and not a single one was omitted. When he realized that there was no response from all those gods, he thought 'I remember that my father, the good King Hezekiah used to quote the verse from the Bible, *In your distress when all these things are come upon you . . . you will return to the Lord your God* (Deut. 4:30). So now I will call upon Him. Perhaps He is different from all the other gods, and He will save me.'

However, before Manasseh began to pray to God, the ministering angels sealed all the gates of heaven to prevent the king's prayer from reaching up to God's throne. The angels then went to God and said, "Lord of the universe! How can you regard the prayer of this wicked man who blasphemed You, who set up idols in Your holy Temple, and who murdered Your prophet?" God replied, "If I do not accept his act of penitence I lock the gates of repentance against every other sinner who might wish to come back to Me." So saying, He bored a hole beneath His divine throne in order to allow Manasseh's prayer to reach Him.

The king prayed with great fervency, "O God, Thou hast promised forgiveness not for the righteous but for the sinners. I have committed many iniquities and I am now weighed down with sin. Therefore I confess my transgressions, and implore Thy forgiveness. I beg You to save me in Thy mercy, and I will praise Thee continually. Thine is the glory, Amen." Manasseh's prayer was accepted by God, and a wind came and carried the king back to Jerusalem" (*Yeb.* 49b; *Ruth Rab.* 5:6; *J.T. San.* 10:2, 28:3).

*   *   *

The story of Isaiah's martyrdom and the account of the angels' intervention to block Manasseh's prayer have no warrant in the biblical record. However, there is a reference to Manasseh's captivity and his prayer of penitence in 2 Chronicles, 33:11–20. Nevertheless, the first piece of folklore which tells of Manasseh's murder of Isaiah is consistent with the picture we have of the king's evil character, while the second part which tells of the king's penitence illustrates an important theological concept which is the real teaching of the midrash.

That teaching relates to repentance and its extraordinary power. Obviously, it is that which is at the heart of God's reply to the angels. Judaism is an optimistic religion which teaches that man, so long as he is alive, can always find the power to improve himself. Indeed, throughout his life he is never finished because of his potential for change and improvement. The miracle of repentance is that by an act of free will a man can alter the entire direction of his life. In the Jewish religious calendar a special period of the year is set aside when the individual is encouraged to engage in self-examination, repentance and personal renewal. But ideally, man is called upon to repent all the time.

The steps in an act of repentance are basically three. Recognition of past faults, regret in having been guilty of such sins, and a firm resolve that they will not be repeated. In Judaism no agent is required to serve as an intermediary between God and man. The sinner faces the challenge of repentance in a direct and personal spiritual encounter with God in the light of the highest religious truths taught in Judaism.

Furthermore, Judaism teaches that no matter how heinous the sinner's former conduct may have been, the gates of sincere repentance are always open. It is as if God waits for the sinner's return and gives him the inner power to change.

31

The Forbearance of God

Before God destroyed the world by bringing the flood, He gave the people a very long time in which they could repent and improve their ways. Thus, the rabbis observe that there were ten generations from Adam until Noah, to show how patient God is, waiting for the sinners' repentance. But things went from bad to worse, and the generation of Noah was totally evil, corrupt and violent.

Nevertheless, God still did not bring on the flood until he had given them a further chance to heed Noah's warnings. For as long as one hundred and twenty years, Noah, the only righteous man in his generation, continued to rebuke the people for their evil ways and warned them of impending disaster should they not repent. Even when God commanded him to make the ark in which he and his family would survive the flood, Noah took a very long time to finish the job. He reckoned that when the people would see him making the ark they would take his warnings more seriously.

So first of all he planted cedar tees. When the people saw him doing this they asked, "Why are you planting these saplings?" Noah told them, "Because I will need the wood to make a big ark." The people then wanted to know why he would need an ark, and he told them, "If you do not mend your evil ways then God will send a disastrous flood which will destroy all living things." When the people heard this they scoffed at Noah and called him a simpleton. The same thing happened each time they saw Noah watering his young trees. They asked the same questions and received the same answers; Noah became the target of their derision. Finally, after many years, the trees had grown tall and strong and were then ready to be cut down for timber. Noah went about his work slowly, very slowly, cutting down and smoothing the boards.

"Why all this heavy work?" the people asked him mockingly.

"I am going to make an ark in which to escape the great flood which God is about to bring to destroy you all because of your wickedness."

But the people went on scoffing him for his simple naivety. They refused to believe him and even threatened to break up his ark. Finally God commanded Noah to bring in the animals who were to survive and to enter the ark with his family, for the great flood was about to begin (*Mid. Tan.* 58).

*   *   *

This midrash is interesting in several different aspects. Here we shall mention only two of them. The first is that our midrash attempts to counter the argument that Noah was not such a "righteous man" as might be thought from the complimentary description he enjoys in the Bible (Gen. 6:9). The criticism levelled against him is that he did nothing to try to save his fellow man. At least the Bible is quite silent about that. He alone was saved, together with his immediate family. But what of the others? Did Noah show any concern for their terrible fate? Surely he could have appealed to God in their behalf, even as Abraham did in a similar situation when he learned of the impending disaster which was to overtake the people of Sodom and Gomorrah. There the Bible eloquently describes Abraham's passionate and lengthy appeal to God in his attempt to save the people. But in the story of Noah the Bible does not record one single word of intercession from Noah; as though he was totally unconcerned with the impending universal destruction.

Our midrash is sensitive to this criticism and almost re-writes the biblical story. At least it fills in some serious gaps by giving the reader a fuller and more charitable portrait of Noah's character. The midrashic folklore does not accept that just because the Bible is silent on the matter then it must follow that Noah remained unmoved by thoughts of the disaster of the approaching flood. On the contrary; if the Bible describes Noah as a "righteous man" it must mean that he was very concerned with the fate of his fellow men and that he would try to do everything he could to save them by getting them to repent and to mend their ways. For a "righteous man" is always involved in human affairs and will never adopt the attitude of "I'm all right Jack!" leaving the rest of his society to suffer. So in fact, says the midrashic folk story, Noah acted like any other biblical prophet in his efforts to preach and to teach, to rebuke and to warn his contemporaries of the disastrous results which would follow if they remain a corrupt society. Of course, none of this is explicit in the Bible story. But as we indicated, that does not worry the author of the midrash who is not really interested in the historical account of Noah and the flood. His consideration here is only with the ethical character of Noah and the justification for his designation as a "righteous man." If this is how the Bible describes him then Noah must have been active in his efforts to save the society in which he lived, because to be a "righteous man" means to be totally involved in the life and welfare of the general population.

The second point which the midrash makes relates to the theme of repentance and its effectiveness. This subject is treated in the previous story of our collection so we will not dwell on it here at any length. But the matter is made clear in the above midrash. The people in Noah's generation were utterly corrupt, so much so that God decided to bring that degenerate society to an end. But first of all they were given a chance to improve their ways. God is patient. "The mills of God grind slow . . . ." For ten long generations God waited for man to repent. However at the end of that intervening epoch from Adam until Noah, nothing had changed. But even then, after Noah had been forewarned about the coming flood, the folklore tells that one hundred and twenty years elapsed before Noah completed his preparation for building the ark. And all this to give the people an extended opportunity to repent.

The emphasis on this aspect of the rabbinic aggadah again illustrates the central place of repentance in Jewish theology. No sinner, however grievous his sin, is ever deprived of the opportunity to repent. It is never too late. Further, sincere repentance—that which changes life—leads to reconciliation with God. This is the optimistic teaching of Judaism, that the gates to repentance and reconciliation are always open.

32

~

The Golden Mean

When Noah came out of the ark following the great flood he began to cultivate the land and he set about planting a vineyard. One day Satan came up to him as he was working the soil and enquired what he was doing. When Noah told him that he was planting a vineyard, Satan asked what a vineyard was for. "From these plants I can grow grapes and from the grapes I can make wine and other strong drink" said Noah. "I would like to come in as your partner" said Satan, and Noah agreed.

It was Satan's job to fertilize the ground and he decided to do it with the blood of animals. So first he slaughtered a sheep and spilled its blood over the young plants. Then he killed a lion and did the same with its blood. Then he killed a monkey and after pouring its blood on the newly planted vines he slew a pig and used its blood in the same way as before.

Why did he do all that? Because it showed the effect of wine and the power it has. After the first drink a man remains sober and can be as quiet as a sheep. After the second glass he feels stronger, like a lion, and may begin to brag and boast from the courage of his cups. After the third drink he begins to act stupidly, prancing about like a monkey. But he can get even worse since after a fourth drink he can become revolting, rolling about in his filth like a pig. This was the reason for Satan's extraordinary method of fertilization, and it should have been a warning to Noah and his descendants (*Mid. Tan.* 58).

*   *   *

The observation has been made that, like so many other midrashim, the above reflects an aspect of the economic situation of the time. The story is then read as a criticism of those farmers who planted too many vine trees to the neglect of wheat and other basic crops. But we shall comment on the midrash from another perspective altogether.

The question is sometimes asked, "What is the attitude of Judaism towards alcohol?" and similar questions relating to the whole subject of abstinence. At the outset it can be said unequivocally that Judaism has absolutely nothing against drinking wine or other strong drink. On the contrary, the tradition keeps an honored place for wine in religious ceremony. The sanctification of the Sabbath and festivals is properly done with wine, and although other liquids may be used for the havdalah ceremony of farewell to the holy days, it is also best performed with wine. Wine is, among other things, the symbol of blessing, of God's bounty and man's happiness. It is used therefore during the marriage ceremony, at a circumcision, and is rarely absent from a Jewish home because of its frequent use in the religious ritual.

However the rabbinic folk story underlines the lesson that undisciplined indulgence can lead to alcoholism, to a breakdown of the moral character and to other personal tragedies.

Is there an antidote to the sickness or the danger of alcoholism? It might appear that total abstinence is the answer and is also an ideal to be recommended as a preventive measure. Some people might be prepared to go further and even recommend it as a means to personal sanctity. Yet abstinence is not an ideal in Judaism.

The Bible does have a section dealing with the laws and lifestyle of a nazirite who had to abstain from all wine, strong drink and its source. The nazirite was a strict abstainer. Yet the attitude of rabbinic Judaism to the nazirite is ambiguous, to say the least. While the rabbis recognize the fact that in certain situations a man may have to undertake the vows of nazirdom, and that in certain cases abstinence may be a worthy or a necessary exercise in self-discipline, they nevertheless tend to the view that the nazirite has somehow put himself in an unethical situation because he has deliberately rejected some of the permitted enjoyments of life and some of the blessings of the good earth which a beneficent God has provided. Whoever refuses to partake of God's blessing is like a dissatisfied and ungrateful subject who cannot recognize a blessing when it is in front of him. That is why one school of thought actually describes the nazirite as a sinner, and explains the law which obligates him to bring a sin offering on the completion of the period of his vow, by linking his sin to his rejection of the permitted blessing of God. There may be a good and valid reason for a man becoming a nazirite and totally refraining from alcohol. Indeed if he is an alcoholic or succumbs too easily to the temptations of excessive drink, then the only way out is to bend completely in the other direction. This is sound advice given also by the Jewish moralists. But we are speaking here of the ideal in a normal situation. And the ideal is not abstinence. Wine is not only permitted; it is a blessing.

Yet this attitude of Judaism goes hand in hand with a strict warning against indulgence. The rabbinic story with which we began speaks for itself.

What then is the ideal? Clearly it is the ideal of moderation. Maimonides makes moderation an ethical virtue of great importance. In Hebrew it is called the *shvil ha-zahav*—the golden mean. It is a similar ethical value which was elaborated upon by Aristotle and other ancient philosophers as a practical guide to many things in life. Maimonides followed him and insisted that it is the only sensible way for man.

We have been talking about wine and abstinence, and in the course of our discussion we have noted that it is sinful for man deliberately to reject the permitted enjoyments and blessings of life. There is no sin in partaking of them. The sin is in rejecting them or misusing them. This standpoint, for example, informs the Jewish attitude towards sex. Sex is not wrong; only illicit sex is sin. Where early classical Christianity regarded celibacy as the ideal and marriage as a concession to human weakness, Judaism holds that celibacy is wrong and that marriage is one of the great blessings of life. The three ancient civilizations—Paganism, Christianity and Judaism—had different attitudes to the material and sensual pleasures of life. Paganism worshipped it all; Christianity rejected it all as sinful; Judaism accepted it all as neutral. That means that it is permitted, but waiting to be sanctified by law, by ethics and by self-discipline. This applies to sex, to food and drink, indeed to all the physical pleasures of life. It has been said that "Judaism is a cheery creed." This is true only if the "good cheer" is enjoyed within the permitted boundaries. In that case such a description of Judaism is totally valid.

33

The Fear of Heaven

Before Rabbi Johanan ben Zakkai died some of his disciples came to visit him as he lay on his sick bed. When the great teacher saw them he started to cry.

"Our master, light of Israel, pillar of our people and sage of Torah! Why do you weep?" they asked him.

Rabbi Johanan answered, "If I were being led to appear before a king of flesh and blood, who is here today and gone tomorrow, whose displeasure can be averted and whose sentence can be reduced, who can even be pacified by pleadings and by gifts—would I still not be afraid of the outcome? How much more so then when I have to make an appearance before the Supreme King of Kings, the Holy One blessed be He, who is eternal, whose anger can last, and who cannot be won over by words or by gifts! Moreover there are but two ways open before me, one leading to Gehinnom and the other to paradise, and I cannot know where I shall be taken. Shall I not tremble then at the awesome possibilities?"

The disciples listened quietly to their dying teacher, and at the end they asked him for a parting blessing.

The rabbi spoke simply and said, "May it be God's will that you fear Him as much as you fear man."

"Is that all?" the students asked with some astonishment.

"Would that you achieve as much as that" replied Rabbi Johanan. "See what happens when a man is about to commit a sin in secret. He is then at least concerned that no one else sees him. . . . But he ignores the fact that there is always an all-seeing eye which sees everything he does" (*Ber.* 28b).

* * *

This story contains a number of ideas which deal with the rabbinic concept of death. But we will not develop that theme here, especially as the subject is touched upon in a few other stories in this collection. It is sufficient to say here only that classical rabbinic theology is unambiguous in teaching that there is judgment of the individual in life after death. In some way, in some place and in some time, the deceased faces a divine judgment where his life on earth is evaluated for good or ill. This concept is clear in Rabbi Johanan's first reply to his pupils. Moreover, he cannot be certain what the verdict on him will be, and whether his destiny lies in the punishment of Gehinnom or in the bliss of Eden. Undoubtedly, the story teller also wants to make his point, by implication, that if the great Rabbi Johanan ben Zakkai, the light of Israel and the illustrious teacher of Torah, is so fearful about his appearance before the throne of the divine judgment, then how much more should ordinary and less worthy people be concerned about their ultimate fate. In rabbinic theology death is real. But it is not the end of the individual's fate, because that stretches out beyond the grave. From then on everything depends on the judgment he merits in the "heavenly court." On that there is no response from the disciples who accept their master's point of view.

But it would appear from our story that the narrator is also interested in stressing another doctrine. Rabbi Johanan ben Zakkai contrasts an earthly king with the Supreme King of kings. People naturally stand in fear of the former, then how much more so should they stand in fear of the judgment of God? In his parting words to his disciples he emphasizes the natural weakness of man who is afraid of being discovered by his fellow in the act of doing something wrong, yet more often than not he remains unmindful of God's all-seeing eye. The students at first think rather little of their master's blessing. But they are then shown that the master wishes to redeem them of a common human weakness prevalent even among the faithful. People are aware of the visible, but remain unthinking of the great Invisible but Omnipresent and Omnipotent God.

Our conclusion then is that really the main lesson of the story stresses a religious ethic which in Hebrew we call *yirat shamayim*, literally "the fear of (heaven) God." The concept needs just a little more explanation.

Jewish biblical ethics teach two themes to guide man's obedience of God's law and teaching. We love God for His gift of life and all the other blessings we can enjoy. We love God because we can trust in Him as the loving God who knows us and cares for us. Through love of God we aspire to live lives of value and purpose; and in obedience to His law we also come to love our fellow man. The great text, *And thou shalt love thy neighbour as thyself* (Lev. 19:18) is a commentary on the central teaching, *And thou shalt love the Lord thy God* ... (Deut. 6:5).

It might seem that fear of God is opposed to the ideal of love of God. Simply put, we fear an authority because of the power invested in that authority to impose punishment., But surely if we are taught to love God and to obey Him out of love, then there should be no room for fear of Him. That is so. Therefore the literal English translation of the Hebrew phrase *yirat shamayim* is rather misleading. A much better translation is "awe" or "reverence" of God. Knowing that God is all-present, then man is never alone. Knowing that there is "an all-seeing eye, an all-hearing ear and a permanent record of all our deeds" would keep the sensitive man of faith in a state of constant awareness that he is always in the presence of God. His life is then filled with *yirat shamayim*, a reverence for God who is always with him.

In a real sense this teaching is the most comprehensive ideal of religion, and the man who has reached it has grasped ultimate blessing which can come to a man of faith. *Yirat shamayim* is not easy to win. In fact it is one of the most difficult of all religious goals. But for all that it remains the great challenge to the religious seeker. The rabbis are aware of that and that is why they can teach, "Everything is in God's dispensation to give except the gift of *yirat shamayim*" (*Nid.* 16b). Man himself has to struggle hard to get that value for himself in a ceaseless and daily challenge.

It is fitting therefore that the boons we pray for in the beautiful petition before each new month includes the request to achieve a life with *yirat shamayim*. It is so fundamental to the religious life that the great Rabban Johanan ben Zakkai concentrated on that value as the substance of his blessing to his disciples before he died.

34

~

Its Ways Are Ways of Pleasantness

Solomon's Temple was the most magnificent building in the ancient world. Next to its architectural splendor and lavish furnishings, the king's throne attracted the awe and admiration of all the kings and princes of the world.

The throne was overlaid with fine gold and studded with emeralds, beryls, rubies, pearls and many other precious stones. It was reached by six steps and on each step there was a pair of lions and eagles facing each other. There were other animals, all made of gold, which adorned the steps all ascending to the throne, and on the top step there was a dove of peace, holding in its hand the rapacious hawk.

Over the throne itself there was a huge candlestick, with seven branches on each side. The figures of Israel's ancestors were on one side of the candlestick, and the images of Israel's righteous men were engraved on the other side.

The area around the throne also contained special seats for the high priest and his deputy, as well as seventy gold seats for members of the Sanhedrin, who sat before the king as they judged.

Whenever witnesses approached the throne to give their evidence, the machinery was set in motion and the cries of the animals on the steps leading to the throne were simulated. The sudden noises of the jungle would so terrify the witnesses that they were scared to utter any false evidence.

When King Solomon set his foot on the first step on his way up to his throne, one of the animals guarding that step would receive him and lift him to the second step, from which he was raised by a guardian animal to the third step, and so on until he reached the sixth step, when the eagles lifted him onto his royal throne.

There were also seven heralds whose office it was to remind the king of his duty to the people and to his God. As Solomon ascended each step to the throne, the heralds called out the law of the kings and judges: *He shall not multiply horses to himself. . . . Neither shall he multiply wives to himself . . . neither shall he greatly multiply to himself silver and gold* (Deut. 17:16, 17). *Thou shalt not pervert judgment. Thou shalt not respect persons neither shalt thou take a bribe* (Ibid., 16:19).

When he was seated on his throne the great eagle would place the crown on the king's head, and then a dove would take a scroll of the Law from its case and place it in the king's lap. Then finally, a seventh herald would call out, "Know before whom thou standest."

Solomon's throne did not remain long in Jerusalem. The nations of the world coveted it and held it as prize booty. First, it was taken by Shishak, king of Egypt. Then Assyria defeated Egypt, and its king Sennacherib took away the throne. On his way back to Assyria, he set siege to Jerusalem. There at the gates of the city he suffered a defeat and he had to return the throne to King Hezekiah.

Years later, Pharaoh Necho of Egypt took the throne back to Egypt, but when he tried to walk up the steps to the throne, he received a crippling blow on his leg from one of the gold lions. A similar thing happened when the throne fell into the possession of Nebuchadnezzar of Babylon.

Later rulers, such as Darius and Ahasuerus of Persia, heard what had happened to others who tried to sit on the throne and so they refrained even from making an attempt. When the throne fell into the possession of the Greeks, they tried to make a copy, but not even all the skill and wisdom of the cleverest of their artisans could bring them success. After the period of the Greeks, the throne was taken to Rome where it disappeared (*Tar. Sh.*).

* * *

This piece of folklore is typical of the fantastic and imaginative writing which surrounded the personality and the court of King Solomon. The lively inventiveness of the authors is limitless. There is no wealth like Solomon's wealth. There is no wisdom like Solomon's wisdom. There is no power like Solomon's power.

For sure, most of these stories were written at a time when Jews lived under alien rule and suffered cruel oppression and exile. It is significant that the authors found refuge in their dreams and in their literary inventions from which they fabricated rhapsodical pieces of a fabulous past glory.

In the legend we read that conquering kings cannot use the magical throne. The throne thus becomes a symbol of the ultimate sovereignty of the Jewish people. They may be conquered and their treasures taken away, but their tragedy is limited in time. The day will come when Israel will be redeemed and its treasures restored. Meanwhile no other ruler can take Solomon's place. His throne remains unique.

All this is easily understood. Yet the folklore we have retold here contains one or two other ideas which are important.

We note that at the top of the throne there is a dove of peace, which holds captive the predatory hawk. The final step to royalty and the ultimate goal of government are symbolized by the defeat of evil and the supremacy of peace. All Solomon's wealth and glory must reach towards peace.

A similar dove of peace flies down to place a Torah scroll into Solomon's lap. There is no Jewish sovereignty without the law of God. But the bearer of the Torah is again the dove of peace, because true religion is a religion of peace. To connect the Torah with war, aggression or destruction is sacrilege, and those who selectively quote the Bible to sanction the use of the bloody sword make a travesty of the Torah teaching. Those passages in the Bible which seem to sanction aggressive war have to be interpreted against their early historical background. And even then they are the troublesome exceptions to the mainstream teaching of Torah whose *ways are ways of pleasantness and all its paths are peace* (Prov. 3:17). Torah can be carried only by peace.

But justice also has a central role in the imagery of Solomon's throne. So there is a place for the judges of the Sanhedrin, and a fearful warning against false witnesses.

Then we have the picture of the heralds who recite before Solomon the laws which are to remind him that he is to rule with personal modesty and with equity. Finally, even as Solomon sits on his throne, a herald calls out to him that he is to remember that he is always in the presence of God.

So in spite of all the power and glory which the folklore fancifully describes, it places the spiritual and moral values in the center of the picture. Somewhere here there is also a lesson for the modern sovereign State of Israel.

35

~

Whatever God Does
He Does for the Best

Once, when he was on a journey to a distant town, Rabbi Akiba stopped at an inn and sought accommodation for the night. But he couldn't get in. "No matter" he said. "Whatever God does He does for the best." He went on for a short distance and came to a field where he decided to settle down for the night. Akiba had with him a donkey on which he rode, a cock to wake him at dawn, and a lamp to light his way. In the middle of the night a lion killed his donkey, and a little later a wild cat ate his cock. Akiba resigned himself to his loss and said, "Whatever God does He does for the best." But that wasn't the end of his troubles, for soon after that a strong gust of wind blew out his lamp, and Akiba was left in darkness. Again he comforted himself with the thought that whatever God does is for the best.

Next morning he learned that during the night a gang of armed robbers had descended on the town and attacked the inn where he had been refused accommodation, murdering some of the guests and robbing all of them. "See" said Akiba, "had I been given a place to sleep in that inn I would also have been a victim. Or had the ass brayed, the cock crowed or the lamp been lit, those murderous robbers would have been advised of my presence here, and I could have suffered the sad fate of the townsfolk" (*Ber.* 60b).

*   *   *

Rabbi Akiba, the great second century teacher, was one of the most famous and important of all the talmudic masters. He was not only prominent in his legalistic authority, but also in the formulation of a number of theological concepts, particularly those touching on free will and human destiny. He is the author of the famous aphorism, "Everything is foreseen; but free will is given" (Avot 3:19). The rabbi holds on to both horns of the dilemma. On the one hand, God in His omniscience knows everything that will happen, as if there is no past, present or future in His sight. But his foreknowledge of what is to happen is non-determinative, and man is given freedom of will to act in one way or another. The subject raises many questions with which Maimonides dealt at very great length. God's knowledge is of a different kind, and Maimonides insists—as did Akiba, one thousand years before him—that God's knowledge is non-determinative. Man's freedom of will is always a basic principle in Judaism.

However, our story seems to deflect from this teaching by suggesting that all the things that happen are somehow engineered by God. This time, by a beneficent God who arranges for all sorts of things to happen in order to keep Akiba safe. There is no way of knowing how much of the story is historical and how much is fabulous. That question is interesting, but not important. What is important is the moral of the story. And this is the belief that everything that happens, happens not only with the knowledge of God, but also through His will. The doctrine falls under the classical theory of divine providence. There is little doubt that rabbinic theology, by and large, has a place for the belief in divine providence and taught that God controls all the affairs of man. Not only the affairs of nations on the large map of human civilization, but also the daily happenings of the individual man. At all events this seems to be what Akiba is saying when after all the things that happened to him he says, "Whatever God does He does for the best."

Now this belief in divine providence is a very hard teaching to accept, and although it undoubtedly has a place within the totality of rabbinic theology, it may be argued that there is substantial room for doubt that it belongs to the mainstream of Jewish doctrine. If anything, Judaism's insistence on free will and its corollary that the world is based on justice—leading to the conclusion that a man is rewarded or punished somewhere, somehow, as a result of his actions committed by his free will—all point to a religious philosophy which has little room for the doctrine of divine providence. This latter notion is too deterministic; too fatalistic. Islam holds firm to such a deterministic philosophy. Everything is the will of Allah, and a man's fate is even *makhtub*—written on his forehead. Calvanistic Christianity is similarly deterministic since it is held that everything that happens to a man takes place through a controlling divine Providence. There are many Jews—among them many scholars—who would argue that the theory of an actual working daily divine providence also has a place in Judaism. There are enough biblical texts to support such an idea. We even have the famous prayer on Rosh Hashanah and Yom Kippur, known as *Unetaneh Tokeph*, where the worshipper says, "On the New Year it is written and on the Day of Atonement it is sealed, who shall live and who shall die; who in his appointed time and who not in his appointed time . . . ." An earlier generation of Jews frequently used the concept of events being what they called *beshert*, i.e., finally determined by a higher power. Therefore we ourselves can do nothing about it. But all these arguments can be debated. Biblical stories and texts are always subject to interpretation, and this certainly would include an analysis of the historical, social and theological backgrounds of the text. Such an examination may show that the concept of divine providence, at least with its deterministic implications, is not necessarily supported. Again, the prayer *Unetaneh Tokeph* with its apparent fatalistic ideas, need not be accepted as a serious prayer. Its legendary history has certainly added to its popularity. But for all that, it is a meditation; not a prayer. And the meditation is significant and certainly in its place on the High Festivals. It is a meditation on the uncertainties in life. No one knows what is going to happen to him in the next year. The only certainty in life is its uncertainty. Therefore it is good to ponder the question, "Who will live and who will die . . . ." Finally, the concept of things being "beshert" may just be one of those notions which earlier generations picked up from the cultural environment in the Arab Middle East, or even among the peasant masses in East Europe. There is no conclusive argument to prove that a daily detailed divine providence controlling the affairs of every man, even to the most minute detail, is a universally accepted doctrine of Judaism.

In that case, if it is not God who directs all the affairs of man, what are we to make of Akiba's story with which we started this piece? Here we wish to offer the thought that the story is not an illustration of the belief in divine providence, but an idea which attempts to answer the ultimate question of all monotheistic religion, why God permits evil things to happen. God is believed to be all-good so He should not permit the existence of evil. He is also all-powerful so He can stop bad things from happening. Jewish teachers have always been exercised with this problem, both from the point of view of the national tragedies which befell the Jews and the individually experienced sadness in the life of man. The rabbis offered a number of ideas; not solutions, just observations. Akiba's story can teach us that when a man experiences evil, he is not always in a position to evaluate what happens. His vision is too limited. He can only see the present, and it is only God in His omniscience, who can know man's fate. What happens to a man may have an immediate painful effect, but the ultimate chapter of the story may prove that the event was beneficial because of its happier ending.

This view of course is not the only one found in the sources. There have been various schools of thought on the subject. For example, the second century Rabbi Yannai proclaimed that we can never know why it is that some good men suffer and some evil men can prosper (Avot 4:19). Maimonides argued that we do not know the real nature of the good and the bad so we cannot arrive at a proper conclusion. Nahmanides (thirteenth century) believed that a good man can suffer as punishment for the small amount of bad which he did, while the wicked man may prosper for the small amount of good which he did. Ultimately however, the "account books" of divine justice are opened in the true world after death. That God's justice is experienced in the World to Come is certainly a widespread teaching in classical Judaism.

Akiba's view as illustrated in our story offers an additional and thoughtful notion. It is of course rooted in his strong faith in a God who is totally good, and therefore nothing which is really evil can happen to the righteous. What seems to be evil only appears to be so to the petty and limited vision of man. *Sub specie aeternatis*, from the eternal and universal view of God, all things will work out alright in the end. A similar view was advocated by one of Akiba's predecessors, Nahum of Gimzo, who is said to have popularized the phrase *Gam zu le'tovah*, "This also is for the best."

A modern writer has given the analogy of a fly crawling all over an exquisite piece of sculpture. Imagine the creature's instinct—if a fly has such. It would be uncomfortable crawling through the holes of the eyes and ears, climbing what would seem to be huge mountains and going down valleys and through sharp clefts. It doesn't like it at all. It prefers the simple lines of a straight wall or ceiling. Only the higher intelligence of a human being can understand the beauty of the sculpture with its high and low parts. Another analogy: if we stand too close to a painting we fail to see its beauty and value. We must stand some distance away from it to see it from a proper perspective. So with regard to the trials and sufferings which at times man is called upon to face, his knowledge of the events, in relation to God's knowledge, is like that of the fly's experience of the difficult surface. Or man's limited understanding and small vision is comparable to that of the man who stands with his nose close to the painting and therefore cannot know what he is looking at. All he "sees" is an unintelligible smear of strange colors. Therefore with his typical optimism, which is also an attitude of Judaism, Akiba holds that the only road open for man is one of faith in the belief that "Whatever God does He does for the best!" which means that God knows what has happened and through divine benevolence all things will end up for the good of the deserving individual.

We agree that this philosophy cannot answer all the questions about the existence of evil. As has already been said, Akiba's approach is only one of several different theories. But whatever its philosophical weaknesses, it does have some power to carry man over the chasm of doubt and help him to face life's present pain with faith in the future.

36

~

The Lord Gave and the Lord
Hath Taken Away

One Sabbath as Rabbi Meir was lecturing in the synagogue, his two sons who had been in the house with their mother, succumbed to a serious illness and died. Their mother laid them on the bed and covered them.

After the Sabbath, the rabbi returned home and asked his wife, "Where are the children?" She said, "I thought they were supposed to go to the synagogue." Meir told her that he had expected them to be there but they did not arrive. She then brought him some wine for the havdalah ceremony, and after he had recited the blessings of farewell to the Sabbath, the rabbi again said, "I wonder where they can be!" His wife replied, "I imagine they went somewhere and we shall soon see them." With that, she brought her husband something to eat, and after he finished his meal she said to him, "I would like to ask you a question."

"Of course" said Meir. "What is the problem?"

"Before the Sabbath" she said "someone came and asked me to mind a valuable treasure for him. Now he wants it back. Shall I return it?"

"What a question!" exclaimed the rabbi. "Of course you must return it to its owner."

"Yes" she answered, "I really knew that I must give it back. Just the same I did not want to do anything without your knowledge and consent."

Then she took her husband's hand and led him to the room where the two boys lay dead. She brought him near to the bed and removed the sheet. When Rabbi Meir saw his two dead sons he broke down and wept bitterly. "My sons! My sons! My teachers! My teachers! You were my sons by nature, but also my teachers since you brought me greater understanding of the Torah by your questioning!"

His wife then gently said, "This is what I meant by my question, and you told me that we are bound to return to their rightful owner what he placed in our care." Hearing this, Rabbi Meir proclaimed, *The Lord gave and the Lord hath taken away. Blessed be the name of the Lord* (Job 1:21). [*Mid. Mish.* 31; *Yal. Shim.*]

*   *   *

First, a brief word about Rabbi Meir and his wife Beruriah. They lived in Eretz Israel in the latter half of the second century. Meir was one of the leading scholars of the mishnaic period, before that great work was edited by Judah the Prince in 200 C.E. So weighty was his recognized authority, that in the process of the redaction of the law many of the opinions and rulings in the Mishnah are attributed to him. His legal decisions therefore provided a basis for Rabbi Judah's comprehensive Mishnah.

His wife, Beruriah, was a daughter of the martyred sage Hananiah ben Teradyon who was murdered by the Romans during the Hadrianic persecutions which followed the failed Bar Kokhba revolt. She is one of the most famous women in rabbinic literature, noted for her wisdom and knowledge of the law. At a time and place when the status of women was secondary, her prominence is unique. Our present story is one of several examples in rabbinic folklore which portray the special kind of wisdom and the psychological insights with which Beruriah was endowed.

Basically, the story illustrates an extraordinary attitude to death which is found in Jewish teaching. We don't know the details of the sickness which caused the death of the two boys, although there is no reason to doubt its historicity. Meir looked for them in the synagogue during his Sabbath lecture, so presumably their death was unexpected.

Now one might have thought that Beruriah would have called Meir from the study house when the children died. But she held her peace. Even when her husband returned home, she refrained from telling him the tragic news. She waited until after Meir had read the havdalah and formally bid farewell to the Sabbath before she broke the news.

Why did she do that? Isn't it most unnatural for a mother and wife to keep silent in the face of such a painful tragedy? The answer illustrates a special Jewish approach to death. There are two experiences in our story: one is totally human and the other is religious. One is death, and the other is the Sabbath. And here they both come at the same time. In such a situation the question is, what takes precedence in our concern? Perhaps most people would hold that it is normal, indeed natural and therefore proper, for a bereaved person to concentrate on the death of his near and dear one, and to attend to such matters as have to be seen to in such circumstances. The Jewish religious attitude however, is that the Sabbath takes precedence. The Sabbath spells life; just the opposite of death. Therefore when both enter simultaneously, priority is given to the greater value, which is life and the Sabbath. Of course, because of the first priority for life itself, the Sabbath must be broken to save life. But once life has gone, then nothing may be done which would detract from the sanctity of the Sabbath or diminish from its life-giving joy. This attitude towards death is quite unique. Death as such has no value. Therefore in the situation described in our story, Beruriah insists on maintaining the Sabbath peace and joy for Meir, and she gave him the tragic news only after the termination of the holy day.

This principle also informs many of the laws connected with death and mourning on the Sabbath. Preparations for a funeral are postponed on the Sabbath. Further, a mourner during the first week of intensive mourning following bereavement is exempt on the Sabbath from many of the laws and customs of mourning. Again, all this is to emphasize the forward looking and optimistic emphasis on life which is an important teaching of the Sabbath and therefore a central concept in Judaism.

A second lesson in the story derives from Beruriah's moving anecdote about the man who came to claim his valuable possession which he had deposited with her for safe keeping. The analogy is perfect. God is the Creator and giver of life. He gave the parents beloved children to train, nurture and cherish. Now in His wisdom He takes them back. Just as it is meaningless to question the rightful owner who wants the return of his precious possession, so one cannot question God when he calls back His children from the world in which He placed them temporarily. Further, the quotation from Job is totally appropriate. Job suffered much, including the death of his children; and he accepted this sad fate with the words quoted by Meir and Beruriah. *The Lord gave*, because He is the source of all life. And *The*

Lord hath taken away, because all life is rightfully His to remove by His divine will. *Blessed be the name of the Lord*, since on the strength of the faith that all is done with God's knowledge and love, then even in moments of deepest sadness and bereavement God can be praised. This is a supreme declaration of faith in God and His purpose in which Beruriah and Meir find their consolation.

37

Give Me Friendship or Give Me Death

Honi the Circle Drawer was walking along a country road when he saw an old man planting a carob tree near his house.

"How long will this tree produce its fruit?" Honi asked the man.

"Seventy years" the old man answered.

"And do you expect to live that long to enjoy its fruit?" asked Honi.

"My parents and grandparents planted for me" said the man, "and in the same way I plant for the benefit of my children and grandchildren."

Honi then sat down in a secluded place to eat a little and to rest. He soon dozed off, and when he was in a deep sleep a rock miraculously grew over where he lay, so that he was protected from the elements and hidden from the sight of passers-by. He slept for seventy years, and when he woke the first thing he saw was someone collecting the fruit of a carob tree.

"Did you plant this tree?" Honi asked the man.

"No, I didn't plant it, but my grandfather did" was the reply.

Honi then realized that he must have been sleeping for seventy years. He went to get his donkey which he had left when he sat down for his meal. Arriving at the place where he had left the animal he was amazed to see many wild donkeys running around. They were the issue of the original beast left there by Honi.

Quite disorientated by the strange sights he had seen, Honi went to his home town and to his house. On arriving at the place he asked the young man who greeted him, "Are you the son of Honi the Circle Drawer?" The young man answered, "No I am not. Honi's son is dead; but I am his grandson." At which Honi said, "I am Honi." But no one would believe him.

Honi then went to the study house and listened to the sages discussing points of Torah law. After a particularly involved debate, the leader of the group said, "Now the law is as clear as if Honi had explained it to us." Hearing this, Honi got up and exclaimed, "I am Honi!" The sages looked at him as if he had gone out of his mind; but no one would believe him.

Realizing that he was without friends, and even without respect, the poor lonely and friendless Honi prayed to God, "Dear God! Give me friendship or give me death!" Whereupon Honi the Circle Drawer expired and died (*Taan.* 23a).

*   *   *

We have already explained that in the literature there are two heroes of the same name and that similar stories about a seventy year long sleep are told of both. It may be that they are one and the same man. The trouble is that the first is placed in the sixth century B.C.E. and our present story tells of a Honi who lived five hundred years later. If they are one and the same person, then the legend of the first one is an eponymous legend which has somehow been transferred to a character who was given the name Honi the Circle Drawer because of his popularity as a miracle working saint. At all events, the first century Honi of our present story is a historical personality about whom many stories are told, particularly of his intercession to God to send rain when there was a serious drought. During his prayers he is said to have drawn a circle in the sand and exclaimed, "Sovereign of the Universe! Know that I will not move out of this circle until you send rain to bless the parched land." This is the origin of his designation, "The Circle Drawer."

Obviously his sleep for seventy years is not historical, but a piece of charming folklore. Similar legends are found in the literature of other peoples, starting from the ancient Greeks.

However, we are not so much interested in examining the sources of the story as in exposing the lesson which is taught by the story; and here there are two ethical teachings which are illustrated. First of all, there is the lesson of parental responsibility for the future. This is charmingly pointed out in the old farmer's reply to Honi about the tree he was planting. Of course he is not planting the tree for himself because he does not expect to enjoy its fruit. But he is planting for his children and grandchildren, just as his ancestors planted for him. It is not only true that "the evil that men do lives after them"— the good that they do also lives after them. Further, the legend seems to emphasize the responsibility of each generation so to live that it leaves behind some good for their descendants to enjoy. Our story illustrates this with reference to the gift of the material blessing of the carob tree planted by the old man for the benefit of his descendants. But the tree also symbolizes the spiritual values which ideally should be planted by parents and grandparents for the enrichment of future generations. That man who is able to leave such treasures for the future lives a life which is fulfilled because its meaning and value goes beyond his own life, and happy is the new generation which can draw upon the spiritual treasures left to them by parents and grandparents.

The second lesson is no less significant, and that is the lesson of the importance of friendship. Man is a social animal who cannot live on his own. A hermit's life is unnatural and cannot be maintained. The sages never tired of stressing the importance of acquiring a friend (*Avot* 1:16), and Rabbi Joshua, a disciple of Rabban Johanan ben Zakkai even taught that a good friend is the most precious asset any man can have in his life (Ibid., 2:13). Obviously, the kind of friendship which is taught here is not the kind which exhausts itself merely in attending each other's parties or playing with a tennis partner. That is companionship, at the most. Real friendship enters into life in a much more profound manner, enabling friends to open their hearts to each other, to share life's joys and sorrows as if they were one's own, to cherish the life and dignity of the other as if it were one's own life and dignity. It is the friendship of a David and Jonathan, of a Ruth and Naomi, of a Damon and Pythias. One of the saddest things in life is to experience friendlessness. For Honi that was worse than death. Hence his prayer, "Give me friendship or give me death!" The historicity of the legend is not important. The rabbis loved to tell the story because of its immortal lesson.

38

~

Stars or Deeds?

The great Babylonian scholar Samuel was very friendly with a Gentile astrologer and wise man named Ablet. One day the two were seated on a small hill overlooking a lake when they saw a group of workers going out to cut reeds by the lake. Pointing to one of the workers Ablet said, "That man will not come back alive because he will be fatally stung by a poisonous snake." Samuel said to him, "If he is a Jew he will come back safely."

Some hours later the workmen returned, including the man whom the astrologer said would be killed. Ablet was surprised and went up to the man. He took the large bundle of reeds from off the man's shoulder, and immediately the scholars saw that a snake had been chopped in two by the man's cutting tool.

So Samuel went up to the man and requested, "Tell me what you have done all day." The man told him all about his day cutting down the reeds, and among other things he said, "We workmen all agree to share our food. At the beginning of the meal, each one of us puts his bread into the communal dish, and all would eat from it. Today I saw that one of our company had nothing and the poor man would have been put to shame, so I volunteered to collect the food from every workman. When I reached this man I pretended to take something from him so that he would not feel ashamed."

When Samuel heard the man's account of what had happened he said to him, "You have done a very good thing. And in a case like yours Scripture declares, 'Righteousness delivereth from death' (Prov. 10:2), which means from death itself" (*Shab.* 156b).

*   *   *

This story cries out for an explanation. But first of all a few words about the *dramatis personae* may be in order. Samuel lived all his life in Babylon during the latter part of the second and first part of the third centuries. He was head of the famous academy of Nehardea and later of Pumpeditha. In talmudic literature he is frequently paired with Rav the head of the Sura academy. But while Rav was the acknowledged authority in all ritual questions, Samuel's expertise and authority was acknowledged in matters dealing with civil law. But Samuel's fame was not restricted to his knowledge of the law: he was an outstanding mathematician and astronomer. He is on record as having said that he knows all the paths of the starry heavens as well as he knows the streets of his native Nehardea.

Ablet was a Gentile Babylonian, one of many about whom the Talmud has numerous references. Generally the Talmud refers to them as "Chaldees," a term which is subject to different interpretations. However, the common factor in all of them is that they are wise men; the "philosophers" among the Gentiles. Moreover the term certainly means to describe them as astrologers who claimed to be able to foretell the future by the stars and the heavenly planets. Samuel and Ablet seem to be on very friendly terms, and this no doubt could have been fostered by Samuel's own knowledge of astronomy.

But here the story illustrates a clear distinction between the attitudes of Ablet and Samuel. The talmudic context in which the story is told is a discussion by the rabbis on whether there is any power in the stars to determine one's fate. It is a discussion with wide and deep ramifications which went on not only in the early period of talmudic theology but carried on with even greater intensity during the Middle Ages when most of the Jewish philosophers of the period believed that a man's fate was at least partially determined by astronomical forces. Maimonides (1135–1204) was almost the exception in that he rejected the claim of the astrologers. Man has free will and his destiny is determined by his deeds and not by the stars. This liberal view has its authentic sources in the Bible where the people of Israel are warned not to ape the ways of the heathen. The Jewish faith is based on the firm belief in the One God who established His law on justice and righteousness. The odd chance of a man being born under a certain star can have no ultimate effect on his character, his behavior or his fate. That is the purity of Judaism.

It is free from superstition and from notions which imply that there are hidden forces—for good or ill—which alone decide a man's fate. This is also the concensus of the talmudic rabbis who are discussing the subject when someone tells the story of Samuel and Ablet. The Talmud states there, "Ein mazal le'Yisrael." The fate of the Jew is not determined by the stars. And the story we quoted is offered as an illustration. Ablet is an astrologer who believes in the sole determining power of the stars. Samuel is an astronomer who rejects such an extreme idea. It is a man's deeds and not his stars which finally determine man's life and destiny. Even if the stars do have some sway over man's fate, such a power can be broken as a result of man's behavior. That is why Samuel said to Ablet that if the man in question is an Israelite there is good reason to expect him to do good deeds during the day which will counteract any evil destiny which may be determined by the stars.

In general terms, this is the attitude also of the medieval Jewish philosophers—with the exception, as we noted, of Maimonides who rejects altogether the place of the stars in determining man's fate.

But the story is fascinating from another aspect. When the bundle of reeds was taken from the workman and opened, they found the poisonous snake cut in two. All things being equal, the workman would have been killed by the snake. But he wasn't. The situation was unique and Samuel has to find a reason why the man was saved from death. And he soon finds the reason. The man showed himself to be a sensitive and compassionate human being, and his behavior when he pretended to take some bread from the poor man who had nothing to give to the communal dish showed sensitivity to the poor man's feelings. He had to see that he was not put to shame. That was the greatness of his ethical behavior. Not only that he arranged for the poor worker to eat with the others, but that he made it seem as if the poor worker was also a contributor. In that act he assured that the poor man was not embarrassed.

The story illustrates the rabbinic ethic which warns against what is called in Hebrew, *halbanat panim*, and which means, shaming a man in public. The literal meaning of this phrase is "to make the face of one's fellow man white." The strange term is usually explained in this way. When a man is shamed in public, he is likely to blush, i.e., go red. Then after a couple of minutes the red blush fades away and the face becomes whiter. The rabbis were so emphatic with respect to this teaching that they comment in several places that one who puts his fellow man to shame in public has no portion in the World to Come. To include such a sin among the most heinous offences is indicative of the severity with which the rabbis regarded the sin of *halbanat panim*. Our story tells that the heroic workman not only made it possible for the poor workman to have food—that was charity enough— but he did more: he saw to it that he was not shamed before his fellow workers. That is why Samuel tells the man that he performed a mitzvah. And the mitzvah was such a great one that he was even saved from death for what he had done. It would appear from the story that Samuel probably believed that the stars have some influence on a man's fate, but that his deeds—good or bad—have a more powerful influence. So then, given the situation where the stars determined that the Jewish workman would be killed, it had to be that his escape from death was the result of the man's good deeds. When Samuel discovered what the man had done, his theory of the greater power of deeds over the stars was vindicated.

39

~

On Miracles

The rabbis taught that after God had created the universe and everything in it, He made ten additional things just before the Sabbath. These ten things are very special because they appear in subsequent Jewish history as items in miraculous events. They are the following: the mouth of the earth at the point where Korah and his rebel gang were swallowed up (Num. 16:31ff); the source of the well which provided water for the Israelites as they travelled in the wilderness (Ibid., 21:16ff); the mouth of the ass which spoke to Balaam (Ibid., 22:27ff); the rainbow which appeared after the great flood (Gen. 9:12); the manna which fell from heaven each morning as food for the Israelites in the wilderness (Ex. 16:4ff); the staff of Moses with which he performed all the miracles in Egypt (Ibid., 4:2, 10:13, 14:16); the shamir worm which cut the stones for the Temple altars since no iron instrument was permitted (Ibid., 20:25); the alphabet; the writing tool, and the tablets of stone on which the commandments were cut through on both sides (Ibid., 32:15). Others add to the list the destructive demons, the burial place of Moses (Deut. 34:6), and the ram which suddenly appeared to Abraham at the time of the binding of Isaac (Gen. 22:13). Rabbi Judah adds also the first pair of tongs which had to be miraculously fashioned without the aid of another tool to lift it out of the furnace.

Rabbi Jeremiah offered the following thought: After God had finished the work of the Creation He imposed some conditions on His work. He stipulated right at the beginning that the sea would part

for the Israelites (Ex. 14:26ff), the heaven and the earth would remain silent while Moses spoke (Deut. 32:1), that the sun and the
moon would stand still for Joshua at Gibeon and the Vale of Ayalon
(Josh. 10:12, 13), that the ravens would feed the prophet Elijah (1 Kg.
17:4, 6), that the heavens would open for Ezekiel (Ezk. 1:1), that the
whale would spew out Jonah (Jon. 2:11), that the fire would not harm
Hananiah, Mishael and Azariah (Dan. 3), and that the lions would
not harm Daniel (Ibid., 6) [*Avot* 5:8; *Ber. Rab.* 5:5].

*   *   *

This piece of folklore hides a serious attempt to answer a difficult question in Jewish theology, namely its attitude to the biblical miracle.

Basically, there are three ways in which Jewish teachers have understood the miracle stories. The first and the most obvious—as well
as the simplest—is to accept the Bible record quite literally as the historical truth. That is to say, they all happened as described. So for example, the plagues in Egypt: all the waters turned to blood, and there
were three days of total darkness before the firstborn in Egypt were
slain. So too the waters of the Red Sea parted for the Israelites and
rushed back on the Egyptians, the earth swallowed up Korah's company of mutineers, and Balaam's ass spoke in a human language.
Everything happened as described.

The second method is to describe the miracles as ethically rather
than as historically true. That is, they did not happen as described: in
fact they may not have happened at all. What the Bible gives us is an
allegorical account which has to be interpreted to reveal an inner lesson. Let us again take the plagues in Egypt as an example. The blood
symbolizes the cruelty and the murderous behavior of the Egyptians,
the frogs and the vermin are symbols of the filth and infectious degra-
dation of Egyptian society, the darkness represents the superstition
and the ignorance which was widespread in the land while the slaying
of the first born mirrors the logical end to the national corruption
where the leaders and the high-placed are overthrown.

The above first two methods need not exclude each other, and
can be held by the same teacher. In that case, he will believe in the
historicity of the biblical account as given, but will also treat the text
homiletically to underline its ethical lessons.

But in addition to the above there is a third method which accepts
the biblical story as history but attempts to explain it by giving it a "scientific" rationale. J. H. Hertz, in his commentary to the Pentateuch, is

an outstanding modern example of this approach. So, the plagues in Egypt took place, but there were natural reasons for them. He says, "As everywhere else in the Bible, the supernatural is interwoven with the natural; and the plagues are but miraculously intensified forms of the diseases and other natural occurrences to which Egypt is more or less liable." In connection with the ninth plague, Hertz refers to Professor Mahler who identified the ninth plague with the solar eclipse of March 13th 1335 B.C.E., which darkened Egypt proper but did not extend as a total eclipse to Goshen where the Jews lived.

It is not clear how every miracle recorded in the Bible could be explained, but the attempt is interesting, and in principle this method goes back a long way—as far back as the rabbinic folklore in our present piece.

What is the motivation behind this attempt to explain the miracle? It is really very simple. God established the laws of Nature at the time of the Creation. Those laws are permanent and unbreakable and make it possible for the universe to endure. If a miracle means the suspension of the laws of Nature, then it just could not happen. It would be impossible because it would upset the stability of the created universe founded on the laws of Nature. We cannot accept therefore that the sun and moon could stand still, or the sea divide to make a dry land path in the middle, or the earth to swallow some rebels, or an ass to talk. For those things to happen, it would mean that God's eternal laws of nature would be broken, and that would be the end of God's created universe.

For this reason the rabbis of our midrash are reluctant to accept the miracle as described without trying to offer a thought which they felt would get them out of the difficulty. And so they suggest that God made ten extra things before He finally completed the Creation. So then, when the question is asked how those things could happen if they break the law of Nature the rabbis offer the thought that God made a separate class of things which are, so to speak, governed by a different class of rules and for which He made room at the time of Creation. In this way they happened, not outside the area of strict natural law, but because they were specially created nuances to that law.

This approach has, in general, informed Jewish theology. In a famous dictum the rabbis declare, "We may not rely on miracles" (*Pes.* 30b). We even find criticism of a man for whom it was thought that a miracle had been done (*Shab.* 53b). Further, the rational rabbis were so distrustful of "miracles" that they suspected them of being tied up with witchcraft and prohibited anyone having benefit from them (*Taan.* 24a-b). Similarly, the great masters of Jewish philosophy, led by Moses Maimonides (twelfth century) minimized the place of the miracle in Jewish theology. Where other religions are in fact based on a miracle, Judaism regards it as a very peripheral concept and not at all essential for the Jewish faith.

One final observation may be in order. Thus far we have discussed the miracle in its plain sense as a supernatural phenomenon which breaks or suspends natural law; or as we saw above is in a separate category of specially created phenomena. But there is another kind of "miracle" which is far removed from all that. That is the miracle of birth, of life itself, of daily existence, of the power of the human spirit by which a man is able to perform the most extraordinary acts of courage. Recognition of this kind of miracle is at the very center of the religious life.

40

～

Voices from the Dead

The following stories are uncanny, but they are told in the Talmud in the most matter of fact way as part of a discussion on whether the dead have any knowledge of the living.

One day, shortly before Rosh Hashanah in a year of drought, a man gave a sum of money to a poor beggar. His charitable act so embittered his nagging wife that he ran away from home and took refuge—of all places—in a cemetery. During the night he heard two spirits conversing with each other.

"Let us take a little journey to the other side" said one of them, "and learn what fate is decreed for the world in the new year."

"I would rather not go" said the other, "because I was buried in coarse reed matting. But you go and tell me what you find out."

So the first spirit went off and on her return she reported what she had heard. "Whoever sows after the first rains will have his seeds destroyed by the hail." When the henpecked husband returned he waited until after the latter rains before sowing his seed while everyone else put in their seeds immediately after the first rains. As a result his plants were the only ones which survived the hailstorms.

Next year he decided to do the same, and he hid in the cemetery before Rosh Hashanah.

"Come with me and let us hear what is decreed for the new year" urged the first spirit.

"Do you go alone, because I am buried in coarse reed matting" said the other. "But tell me what you learn."

When the first spirit came back she confided to her companion, "I heard that this time whoever sows after the second rains will have his seed killed by the frost."

The man heard the report and went home. That year, hurt by the experience of the previous year, everyone waited until after the second rains to sow their fields. But the man from the cemetery sowed his immediately after the first rains. When the frost came all the other fields were blighted, but that man's plants were already much stronger and were able to withstand the frost. His were the only plants to survive.

Our next story is told in the same context. The father of Samuel was entrusted to look after the savings of the widows and the orphans. The good man died suddenly before he could tell his son where he had secretly hidden the money. Being unable to find it, Samuel was worried about the poor owners of the money and he feared that he could be accused of theft. So having no other recourse he went to the cemetery to ask the spirit of his dead father where he had hidden the money. When he saw his father's spirit he was surprised to see that he was half weeping and half laughing. "Why are you weeping?" he asked him.

"Because I know that you will soon die" he answered.

"Then why do you laugh?" asked the son.

"Because you are so highly esteemed in this place" was the reply.

Then Samuel asked his father where he had hidden the money of the widows and the orphans.

"Dig up the ground close to the shed of the millstones. There you will find three layers of money. The top and the bottom layers were mine, and they are now therefore yours. The middle layer is the money of the widows and orphans." He hid the money in that way, because if thieves found it, they would quickly run off with the top layer; while if rodents would gnaw away at it, they would more likely scamper off with the bottom layer. In either case the deposits of the poor would be secure (*Ber.* 18b).

*　　*　　*

Like most religious systems, Judaism also discusses the subject of life after death. There are so many ideas on this matter that it would require a very lengthy work to sort them out in any systematic fashion. There is also the important consideration of foreign influences which have entered into the treatment of the subject in Jewish literature, so

that it is necessary to separate what belongs to authentic and normative Judaism as distinct from notions which have seeped in from
Babylonian, Greek and other pagan cultures.

However, in spite of that cautionary remark, it is possible to make
a statement which will correctly describe the general attitude to the
subject as found in mainstream Judaism. We can divide our observations into two parts. The first is that Judaism holds to the belief in life
after death. It is not our concern here to argue whether this means
physical life in any material shape, or simply a soul life of the pure
spirit. Nor are we concerned here with the question whether life after
death means that the individual becomes part of a universal soul life,
or a separate personal existence. All that we need to note here is that
Judaism maintains the belief that there is some form of existence
which continues beyond the death of the physical body. Jewish philosophers have consistently submitted to these teachings based on rational as well as metaphysical grounds. But this belief is also strongly
related to the concept of reward and punishment, a doctrine which
extends the balance sheet of life on earth to the beyond where the accounts of a man's life on earth receive their final justification and
recompense.

Having said that, it is difficult to go any further with any degree of
certainty. So the second observation we can make is that in Judaism
there is a healthy reluctance and even an explicit discouragement to pry
into the mysteries of the next world. The Bible gives a stern warning
against communicating with the spirits of the dead (Deut. 18:9–12).
King Saul was emotionally disturbed when he contrived to commune
with the spirit of the prophet Samuel through the medium of the witch
of Endor (1 Sam. 28). Before that, he had endeavored to rid the country of such practices. The conclusion we can come to is that, having laid
down the principle doctrine that there is life after death, Judaism will
then actively discourage any attempt to calculate the mysteries of such
an existence. It is possible; but it is spiritually unhealthy and morally
dangerous. The folklore with which we began is quite unrepresentative
of Jewish teaching; and in any case the behavior of Rabbi Samuel is told
within the context of his personal emergency situation.

Of course there is also a mystical stream in Jewish teaching. Kab-
balists relished that aspect of Judaism. But most rabbis opposed the
study of Kabbalah except for the mature scholar. And even so they
often argued that the chief characteristic of Judaism is anti-mystical
and more rational. It says less about the other worldly and esoteric,
and prefers to concentrate on the practical this-worldly duties of
man. Generally speaking, Judaism is relatively free of demons, ghosts,

spirits and such phenomena. Of course there are references to them in our literature. But they can be read in one of two ways. Either they are fiction, like the modern writings of I. B. Singer who wrote superb fiction but no serious theology; or as in the stories quoted above, where they are primarily meant to show that the spirit world is real. But they cannot be read to encourage communication with the dead. The stories are extraordinary, bizarre, and most certainly non-didactic. They may point to a theological idea but do not offer guidance for real life. Folklore never teaches law or practical Judaism. For that we have to go to the legal sources, and there normative Judaism will underline the classic text of the Bible which is still the standard bearer of Judaism in this matter. A key text is the famous verse, *The secret things belong to the Lord our God; but the things that are revealed belong unto us and to our children forever, that we may do all the words of this law* (Deut. 29:28).

41

~

When will the Messiah Come?

Rabbi Joshua ben Levi once met with Elijah the prophet and in the course of their conversation he asked, "When will the Messiah come?"

"Why don't you go and ask him yourself?" said Elijah.

"Where can I find him?" the rabbi wanted to know.

"You will find him sitting at the gates of Rome" answered Elijah.

"And how will I recognize him?" Rabbi Joshua asked.

"You will see him among the poor, the afflicted and the diseased, binding up their wounds. However while all the others bind an entire area covering several wounds with one bandage, the Messiah dresses each wound separately."

With this information Rabbi Joshua took himself off to Rome, and there at the gates of the city he saw the Messiah attending to the poor and the sick, just as Elijah had described.

"Peace to you my master and teacher" said Joshua.

"Peace to you, son of Levi" answered the Messiah.

"Master, when will you come to redeem us?" the rabbi asked.

"I will come today" the Messiah answered.

Rabbi Joshua ben Levi returned home, and soon afterwards he again met with Elijah the prophet.

"Did you speak with Messiah?" the prophet asked.

"I did" replied the rabbi. And he reported on the conversation. But then he added, "The Messiah lied to me. He promised that he would come 'today'; but he didn't come."

The prophet answered, "What he meant was 'today' if the people would but hearken to God's voice" (Ps. 95:7) [*San.* 98a].

*   *   *

There the story ends, and it is open to examination at several points since it seems to teach some important things. But first of all, a word or two about Rabbi Joshua ben Levi. We have already met this great personality in our collection of folklore. He lived in the Holy Land during the first part of the third century, and was therefore one of the first of the post-Mishnah scholars. Nevertheless some of his teachings are in fact recorded in the Mishnah. Although his name frequently appears as the author of legalistic rulings, his fame lies in the area of *aggadah* or folklore. Like several of his colleagues, Rabbi Joshua was a great mystic who pondered on the questions of life after death and the World to Come. The Talmud records that, like several of his colleagues he often met with Elijah.

This meeting of the rabbi with the prophet Elijah has been variously interpreted. The most obvious explanation is that it takes place in a dream. This explanation is in good company with Maimonides' treatment of the prophetic experience where prophets hear the word of God. Another reasonable explanation suggests that meeting with Elijah is a phenomenon which takes place in the deep sub-consciousness of the rabbi after a period of intensive spiritual exercises. Caught up in that kind of sublime emotional feeling the rabbi would then experience a vision which, for him at least, is subjectively true. The times were hard, and fervent hope for redemption was always on the mind and in the heart of the Jewish leader. In such a context a visionary meeting with the forerunner of the Messiah becomes psychologically real.

But now, back to the lessons to be learned from the story we have cited. First of all, is the belief in the coming of the Messiah. In classical Jewish theology there is a certain ambiguity. Is it hope in the development of a messianic period suggested by the oft repeated prophecy, *And it shall come to pass in the end of days . . .* ? (Cf. Isa. 2:2). Or is the messianic hope invested rather in the appearance of an individual, a divinely sent messenger or "anointed one"? Of course the two theories do not necessarily cancel each other out, since the former can be thought of as introduced by the latter. Nevertheless, there has always been a significant difference in the two approaches to the messianic belief. The first, the belief in a messianic age, is thought of in terms of the progressive development of historical forces leading to the elimination of evil, and the prevalence of the good. The second belief, the belief in a messianic personality, is thought of more clearly in terms of the miraculous intervention of God to redeem Israel, restore the exiles to the holy land, and bring final salvation and perfect happiness to all mankind.

As can be readily seen, the story of Rabbi Joshua ben Levi is a story involving the belief in a personal Messiah, and there is little doubt that this was the prevalent faith of the Jews in the first centuries. Let us come to another lesson implied in the story and which is very well worth noting.

The Messiah sits at the gates of Rome binding up the wounds of the injured outcasts of society. It seems that what is here intended is the portrayal of the Messiah, even before his formal coming, as being very involved in the world's afflictions. In other words, although he has not yet come in his capacity as the declared Messiah, he is present among mankind helping to relieve the pain and the afflictions of a bruised humankind.

But the most important part of the story is the Messiah's reply to Rabbi Joshua, as interpreted by Elijah. The Messiah will come 'today,' that is, as soon as possible, if the people obey God. The meaning is clear. It is the actions of the people, their obedience to the will of God, which will attract and speed up the coming of the Messiah. In other words, the people as a whole can bring about the messianic age in history once they obey God's teaching. The emphasis has now been shifted from the miraculous appearance and intervention of a messianic figure and placed on the concerted actions of all men of good will who can initiate a new age of redemption through the force of their conduct.

A nice gloss was once given to the story and its interpretation by Chaim Arlosoroff, a leader of the Zionist Movement in the first decades of the century. He wrote in his memoirs that when he was a young boy he once asked his grandfather to explain the story to him. "I really cannot understand why the Messiah didn't come, after promising Rabbi Joshua that he would come straight away. What is he waiting for?" asked young Arlosoroff. And his grandfather answered, "He's waiting for you, my child." In a real sense he is waiting for every Jew, and indeed for every good person, to assist in his coming, by contributing a little to the establishment of a society of peace, a society redeemed of evil, a refined and ethical society which is on the way to develop for itself the golden age of a messianic era. As far as the Jew is concerned, this concept of the messianic belief which has always been centered in Jewish teaching, is the great challenge of being a Jew, and is perhaps the clue to the mystery of Jewish history and survival.

42

Clothes for the Messiah

On the day when the Temple was destroyed by the Romans, a man who lived many miles from Jerusalem was ploughing his field. In the middle of a furrow his ox lowed. Just then a stranger passed and heard the animal.

"Who are you?" he asked the farmer.

"I am a simple Jew" answered the man.

"Then you must unyoke your ox and stop ploughing."

"But why on earth should I do that?" the farmer asked.

"Because your people's Temple has just been destroyed" said the stranger.

"And how do you know that?" queried the Jew.

"I know from the lowing of your animal" the man answered.

The farmer released his animal from the plough, and the two went on talking when suddenly the ox lowed again.

"O Jew!" cried the stranger. "Put back the reins on your beast and bind it again to the plough. For the Messiah has just been born; the savior of Israel!"

"What is his name?" asked the Jew.

"His name is Menachem."

"And what is his father's name?"

"Hezekiah."

"Where does he live?"

"He lives in the capital town of the Arava in Judea" answered the man.

The Jew was full of questions which the unknown stranger was able to answer straight away. The farmer then left his home and his fields; he sold his ox and his ploughshare and with the money he bought infants' clothes which he peddled in all the towns on his way to the Arava. His purpose was to find the newborn Menachem. When he came to the town where the baby lived with its mother, all the other mothers came out to buy clothes for their children. All, that is, except Menachem's mother. The other women called out to her, "Mother of Menachem! Mother of Menachem! Come out and buy clothes for your baby!" But the mother refused and seemed very distraught. "Why are you so upset?" they asked her. And she answered, "Because on the day my baby was born, our Temple was destroyed." The man who was selling the children's clothes went up to her and said, "Just as the Temple was destroyed on the day of his birth, so at that time someone was born who is destined to redeem Israel. Take comfort in that thought. Now come and buy some clothes for your baby."

"But I have no money" said the mother.

"What do I care for the money?" answered the man. "Come, take what you want, and I will come back in a few days and you can pay me."

Sometime later the man returned to that town to find out how the infant was growing and what was happening to it. When he came to the house he asked the mother, "How is your baby?" She then told him, "After you saw me last time, the strong winds of a severe tempest swept him out of my arms and carried him away. I don't know where to" (*Jer. Ber.* 5a; *Lam. Rab.* 1:51).

*   *   *

This is indeed a very strange story which cries out to be interpreted, and without any doubt it can be subjected to a wide variety of different interpretations and special emphases. There is only one implied lesson which is fairly clear. The message of the story is connected to the Jewish national experience and the destruction of the Temple, and the exile. This led to a feeling of despair among wide sections of the community. Against that sombre background of national gloom our *aggadah* offers a note of hope and optimism.

The first picture we have in the story is that of the farmer at his plough. Presumably, he does not know about the destruction of the Temple because of the distance from Jerusalem. The stranger is described in the sources as an "Arab." At all events, he is not a Jew, and he knows about the destruction of the Temple from the lowing of the ox. The ancients firmly believed in the signs offered by all kinds of natural phenomena such as the stars, the moon and even animal sounds. It is interesting that the Jew accepts the medium of his information without any question. The instruction to cease ploughing is a proper one, since the Jew has to show some appropriate sign of mourning.

Then when the ox lows a second time, the "Arab" tells the Jew that the Messiah of Israel has been born. He gives some information and an instruction. The information is that the child's name is Menachem, which means "comforter." That lesson is important. The destruction of the Temple is not the end of the Jewish people. From out of the ruins of the catastrophe Israel will find the strength to gather together the elements of its national and religious life and will be able to rebuild. All is not lost. Far from it, for God has not forsaken his people. In the rabbinic language of a third-century midrash, "On the day of the destruction of the Temple the Messiah was born." That lesson, or rather the implications of the lesson, were absolutely crucial for the continuity of the Jewish people at a time when they might have been submerged in a sea of despair.

The stranger gives the Jew an instruction, to tie up his ox again to the plough. This indicates that the proper course of action for the Jew is to continue working—even in the apocalyptic times of the Messiah. This seems to echo the rabbinic ethic that a laborer caught in the middle of the furrow by the advent of the Messiah, or in the middle of planting a tree when the Messiah comes, should first of all finish the work he is doing and then go out to welcome the Messiah. The point is that the rabbis were concerned to ensure that the normal life of the people should proceed. Only on that basis could they hope that the traumatic national experiences would be overcome and that the Jews would face the future with the courage and determination which would eventually bring them to a happier period of national revival. So the emphasis is on the pursuit of the normal and necessary duties of daily life. The Messiah is in the world: but the Jew has his work cut out—to continue ploughing!

However, the Jew does not follow the advice of the stranger. He leaves his daily routine and his work station. He is more interested in looking for the Messiah. So he sells his ox and his plough and goes out to search for him. The mother of the baby and the other townsfolk are unaware of the birth of the Messiah. That is a mystery. But even the man who believes that he knows the child's identity is finally taught that the progress of the Messiah and his advent on the stage of history must remain a mystery to him also. That is the meaning of the report that the child had been swept away by the winds.

One has to ask what the effect of the story would be on its listeners. Essentially there are two lessons which they could gain from it. First, the encouragement that the Messiah has been born. They could interpret that notion in any way they could. But basically, it meant at least one thing for all schools of thought; viz., that the seeds or the elements of redemption have been created by God and are in existence. Second, and by no means less important, is the emphasis on the present and every-day duties of the Jew. His is not the task to enquire and to search for the Messiah or messianic signs. All efforts in that direction will fail. In Jewish history there have been over thirty false messiahs—eleven of them in the period following the destruction of the Temple. In each case the advent and the failure of the false messiah brought nothing but disaster to the Jewish people. Responsible teachers not only disparaged all attempts to support messianic pretenders; they also discouraged efforts to calculate the time when the Messiah would appear. The messianic age or the messianic personality are mysteries in the hands of God alone. The proper task of the Jew is to proceed as conscientiously as he can with his daily life and responsibilities. When carried out to the greater benefit of his community as a whole, then he contributes something to the improvement of society and thus helps bring forward the ideal age of the Messiah.

43

Adventures into the Occult

Four scholars studied the occult and discussed the deep mysteries of the Creation and the heavenly chariot of Ezekiel 1. The four were Ben Azzai, Ben Zoma, Elisha ben Abuya and their leader and teacher Rabbi Akiba. The latter directed their speculations and warned them that when they reach the heights of their spiritual exercise and they arrive at the pillars of translucently pure heavenly pillars of marble they should not call out "Water! Water!" for they would be mistaken. Ben Azzai looked at the mysteries and died an early death. Ben Zoma reflected on them and lost his sanity. Elisha ben Abuya thought about them and lost his faith. Only Rabbi Akiba handled the experience and survived with unimpaired health, wisdom and faith (*Hag.* 14b).

* * *

This talmudic parable is often quoted to illustrate the classical Jewish approach to investigation into the esoteric mysteries of life. Seen in that way, it has been correctly interpreted.

The four characters in our story lived in the second century and were closely connected with each other as teacher and disciples-colleagues. Akiba was the great teacher and guide. Ben Azzai and Ben Zoma were young disciples whose knowledge and erudition both in the fields of *halakhah* and *aggadah* earned them a distinguished place in the history of the rabbinic period, although neither of them was officially ordained. Elisha ben Abuya was a special character whose story has been the subject of numerous studies, as well as historical novels. A later story in this collection will tell how he became a heretic. On account of his heresy, he is not referred to in the talmudic source of our present story by his real name, but by the derogatory nickname Aher which means "the other one." Since, as an heretic, he was virtually ostracized by the rabbis, it follows that his involvement with his three colleagues as related in our story must have taken place before his rebellion against the Jewish faith. Further, from our later story about Elisha ben Abuya it would seem that his heresy was brought on by other experiences, rather than by his excursions into the occult. However, it is likely that his speculations into the esoteric opened the way to his unorthodox thinking.

These four men, relates the Talmud, entered the *Pardes*—literally "the orchard" which is here a metaphor for the occult. Specifically, according to the commentators, this means the study of cosmology, viz., all matters connected with the creation of the universe, and also what is known as *maaseh merkavah*, the subject of Ezekiel 1 touching on "the heavenly chariot," i.e., the mysteries of the divine throne and the chariot which carries it all together with the heavenly court of ministering angels.

There are two things which are noteworthy for our brief discussion. First, something might be said about the historical background of our talmudic story. Second, we ought to address the question of the place of mysticism in Judaism.

With regard to the historical background of the story, it should be noted that all four scholars lived during and after the abortive Bar Kokhba revolt against Rome, which ended so disastrously for the Jewish people. That failed attempt to throw off the yoke of Rome resulted in the slaughter of countless Jews, the enslavement of thousands more, a widening of the exile of Jews to other countries far away from the Holy Land and the further imposition of the most severe decrees against Jewish life including the prohibition of practising the most basic Jewish observances. It was one of the darkest periods in Jewish history. Now in such a time when things seemed at their lowest, the scene is set for mystical speculation. Such exercises are based on the theory that there is quite another world of reality outside the present harsh world of Jewish suffering. It was also natural for scholars and respected leaders to take the lead in such speculation, or at least to be personally involved in searching into the occult. Such a phenomenon existed in many periods of Jewish history when the physical situation of the Jews was extremely hard to bear. We notice the same surge of interest in mysticism in the period immediately after the destruction of the Second Temple, and more particularly in the dark Middle Ages which produced a voluminous esoteric literature. Frequently such speculation went together with messianic movements, as was the case in the first century with eleven false messiahs and in the seventeenth century after the Chmelnicki massacres in Poland with the rise of the Sabbatean movement of the false messiah Shabbatai Zevi. Interestingly enough, the post World War II period also gave rise to a significant surge of new interest in Jewish mysticism with an appreciable number of new publications almost every year, dealing with the Kabbalah and Jewish mysticism. It is suggested, within the framework of the above observation, that the Jewish experience of the Holocaust brought about a diminishing faith in the earlier concept of human progress, or in a world drunk with notions of scientific and material advancement. There was no country so sophisticated, so "cultured," so scientifically advanced as Germany. Yet that same country organized and supported the deliberate slaughter of millions of innocent people. So the material world of reason and scientific progress failed, and the human family, particularly the Jews were the victims. No wonder then that Jewish mysticism became more popular. Every university in the United States which organized courses on Jewish studies had to include a course on Jewish mysticism. Every popular book store stocked books on the subject. Rationalism was temporarily out; and mysticism was in, at least for the time being. So our four rabbis who entered the *Pardes* of deep mysticism were part of a pattern which repeated itself several times in the history of Jewish scholarship.

Now we have to address ourselves to the second point when we ask the question, Is mysticism an authentic element in Judaism? Of course, it all depends on how we define mysticism. If all we mean by this term is that it embraces a belief in a reality beyond the material world, then of course Judaism has a great deal of mysticism. This is experienced every time the Jew performs a commandment with absolute devotion and sincerity and as a result of the observance he feels the spiritual power of the observance in bringing him closer to God. Then he has had a mystical experience. Professor Boaz Cohen, who was professor of Jewish law in the Jewish Theological Seminary taught that there are at least four elements in every Jewish religious action—the legal, the philosophical, the ethical and the mystical. The interested student might like to examine at least some of the main institutions of the Jewish religion and discover those four elements. The obvious cases to check are the Sabbath, Kashrut and prayer. But the same principle will hold for every Jewish religious observance.

Looked at from this angle then we can answer our question in the clear affirmative. Of course there is a large element of mysticism in Judaism. But if mysticism breaks the boundaries of the spiritual emotion and invades the unknown and unknowable areas of the essence of the Divinity then it is arguable that there is little or no place for it in classical Judaism. However advanced the human mind and human knowledge might be, it is still limited and cannot grasp the secrets of the Divinity. Ultimate questions as to the nature of God, how He created the universe, how God began, the nature of life after death, are questions to which the human mind has no answer. The biblical references to a world of angels and the heavenly throne—if taken more or less literally—are also examples of the unknowable, and all efforts to pry into those secrets are wasted effort at the best, and even spiritually harmful at the worst. One of the most extreme forms of such mysticism is found in several ancient manuscripts known under the title of *Shiur Komah* which attempts to describe God in anthropomorphic or human terms. The work even offers descriptions of the limbs of God and their size! God is a kind of superman whose arm can stretch out from the heavens to rescue the people of Israel from Egypt *with a strong hand and an outstretched arm* (Deut. 4:34). Even the divine robe with which God is clothed is described in the most fantastic terms. This example of anthropomorphism gone wild was decidedly rejected by all the rational schools in Jewish thought. And yet there is no doubt at all that even such extreme mysticism is found in the sources from the early talmudic period and onwards.

Our conclusion is that mysticism of this kind, including much of what is described as kabbalistic teaching, does not belong to the mainstream of Judaism. A rabbinic midrash nicely asks the question why the Bible begins with the second letter of the Hebrew alphabet, the letter *beth*. And the answer given is that the letter is closed on the top, on the bottom and at the back. There is only one side open which is in the front. This suggests that when we study the Torah we are not to enquire what is above, what is below and what was before the beginning of Creation. There is only one way open which is to study what is before us, our duties and responsibilities in the here and now.

This rational approach of Judaism is the normative and mainstream school of rabbinic Judaism which has given it the honoured description of a rational religion. There are of course many things which are above and beyond human understanding, so we cannot reason our way to everything we would like to know. On the other hand, there is nothing in Judaism which is against reason.

THE NATIONS

44

~

How Odd of God

Before God gave the Torah to the children of Israel He offered it to the other nations of the world, but they all refused it. The first people whom God approached were the Edomites.

"Will you accept the Torah?" He asked them.

"First of all tell us what is in it" they replied.

"Many laws and teachings" said God.

"What kind of laws? Give us an example" they insisted.

"Well, it is written *Thou shalt not murder*" said God.

"In that case it is not for us" they replied. "How can we possibly live with such a law? Our ancestor Esau was a killer, and Isaac his father promised him that he would live by the sword. We won't have anything to do with your Torah." So God then tried with the people of Ammon and Moab, but with a similar result.

"What's in it?" they asked.

"It is a Torah with many laws including the laws prohibiting adultery and incest."

At this the Ammonites and Moabites were scornful and said, "How can we possibly accept a Torah which denounces our very origins and existence? We owe our very life to the sex acts committed by Lot's daughters with their own father. Your Torah is not for us."

Then God went to the Ishmaelites with the same offer. But when they heard that the Torah contained the law, *Thou shalt not steal* they refused it outright saying that their entire life was built on the basis of theft and robbery.

Finally, God went to the people of Israel, and when He asked them to accept the Torah, they immediately replied, *Naaseh v'nishma*, "We will obey its laws, and we will learn what the Torah is all about." Their reply indicated an unquestioned trust in God and His Torah, and so they committed themselves to its observance even before they learned what laws the Torah contained (*Sifre V'Zot Ha-berakhah*; *Pesikta Rabbati*, 21).

*   *   *

Two things are implicit in this piece of folklore. The first is the idea of universalism. God is concerned about the situation of every nation since all peoples are His creation. He therefore approaches other nations and asks them to receive the Torah. In one way or another, this concept of God's concern for all peoples—not only for Israel—is found again and again in the Bible as well as in rabbinic ethics. In our present context it is seen in relation to the idea that God wants the moral standards of all nations to be raised.

But the nations refuse to accept the Torah. Only Israel was willing and even extraordinarily enthusiastic to receive it. And here we come to a central concept in Jewish theology—the chosenness of Israel, or as it is sometimes called, the election of Israel.

In its simplest form the doctrine means that God deliberately chose the people of Israel for a particular purpose in history. The belief is not so bizarre as it sometimes sounds to the modern ear. God is not only the God of Creation. In theistic religion He is also the God of history who is concerned with the moral development of the world which He created. The atheist who maintains that there is no divine governance in history may point to the lawless state of affairs in many parts of the world. The record of man has been punctuated very frequently by exhibitions of brutality and inhumanity. But the theist is justified in maintaining the belief in the overall improvement in human life, thought and morality, over the ages. True, the development has been slow; at times it has even taken a step backwards in the process. But even taking into account the periods of regression there is little question that in general, man has been elevated over the barbaric savagery of his primitive ancestor. In the story of the rise of man, God uses many agencies to uplift the human spirit. He uses individuals, like the prophets, as His messengers in His divine plan. Holding on to this belief, why then should we exclude the concept that an entire people—in this case the people of Israel—has been divinely chosen as an agency to work as a civilizing force in the history of mankind?

For believers in the concept of the election of Israel, it is the purpose of such election which is all important. This cannot be over-emphasized. Israel's chosenness is not for any temporal power, not for territory and not for wealth. The whole idea of Israel's election is rooted in its ethical meaning, and is connected with the story with which we began. That is to say, the purpose of the chosenness of Israel is exclusively religious. It is to teach the world, through Torah, the truth about the only One God, the brotherhood of man, and the morality of an ordered society. Through such chosenness Israel becomes the religious teacher of mankind. The election of Israel gives no advantages to the Jews; only responsibility.

When we ask, Why Israel and not any other people? the answer is again suggested by our story which can be read as an illustrative comment on a fact of history. The story in our present piece suggests that while all nations had the offer of Torah, only Israel deliberately chose to build its life with that as its guide. In so doing the Jewish people often lived close to the idea of being God's witnesses on earth.

Acknowledging this as an historical fact leads many thinkers to shift the emphasis away from the mystery of a God who chooses a particular people to the historical statement that it was Israel who chose God. Rather than talk of a "chosen people," talk instead of a "choosing people." The picture now is of a people who brought its belief in the One God to other nations and faiths, of a people whose prophets taught the values of justice, compassion and peace, of a people who chose Torah as a way of life, and in the process of living out the details of the Torah brought to all mankind the gift of a moral law.

45

~

When the Angels Stopped Singing

Seven days after Pharaoh had permitted the Hebrew slaves to make their exodus from Egypt, he changed his mind. Gathering together an impressive cavalry he pursued the departing Israelites as they were encamped before the Sea of Reeds. The former slaves felt trapped. They couldn't go forward because of the sea, and they couldn't go backwards because of the oncoming Egyptian army. Then they received their marching orders to go forward into the sea whose waters were then divided allowing the Hebrews to cross safely to the other side. When the Egyptian cavalry drove into the divided waters, their chariots stuck in the mud and the waters rushed back into their natural state, sweeping away Pharaoh and his horsemen as they drowned in the tempestuous waters.

Realizing that they were free at last the Israelites were jubilant and broke into a song of triumph and thanksgiving. But while they were the only ones who sang, they were not the only ones who wanted to sing. The angels also wanted to sing. Before the Egyptians were drowned there was a heavenly debate on how God should deal with them. The guardian angel of Egypt wanted God to deal with them in His attribute of divine compassion. Other angels, led by Michael and Gabriel, urged God to act with His attribute of strict justice. When God agreed to this latter view, and the Egyptians drowned, His ministering angels wanted to break out into song. But they were silenced by God Himself. "This is no time to sing when My creatures, human beings whom I made, are drowning!" This rebuke from God brought the angels to a halt before they could get very far with their singing (*San.* 39b).

*   *   *

This beautiful and well known legend is worth emphasizing because it holds up an ethic which is frequently forgotten; or worse, deliberately brushed aside. The meaning of the story is the obvious one which underlines the concept of the unity and brotherhood of man which is a corollary of the concept of the unity of the One God who is the Creator of all mankind. Judaism teaches the belief in the Unity of God as its first doctrine. But that teaching is meaningless unless it is bracketed with its natural and logical sequel of the fatherhood of God over all mankind.

In the legend, God seems to say, "It is true that the Egyptians deserve the extreme penalty because of their murderous oppression of the Israelites. Therefore I will deal with them with My attribute of Justice." This is recognized. There are times when strict justice is the only right way, for otherwise society would become a jungle of barbaric savages where only the strongest and the most cruel would survive.

But God's rebuke to the angels is a reminder that the death of the enemy is not a proper cause for rejoicing because their destruction is the death of a people who are also the creatures of God. In the talmudic source of the legend, God calls the Egyptians *maasei yadai,* i.e., "the work of my hands; the people I have made." Therefore it is wrong for the angels to sing. It may well be that this is an ethic of perfection, and that it is so ideal that ordinary men cannot be expected to live by it. Perhaps that is why it is only the angels who are told to stop their singing. Moses and the children of Israel—those who actually went through the Egyptian slavery and its cruelty—sang. And they sang their song of praise with great fervor. Yet it is good that the ideal is there. Frequently an ethic is higher than the reach of ordinary folk. Yet it has to be there as a challenge for men to aspire to grasp it. Otherwise the dangerous slide downwards becomes too easy.

The Bible teaches *Rejoice not when thine enemy falleth, and let not thy heart be glad when he stumbleth; lest the Lord see it, and it displease Him, and He turn away His wrath from him* (Prov. 24:17–18). It seems to say the same thing that our legend illustrates.

After Israel's dramatic victory in the Six Day War of June 1967, there was natural and widespread rejoicing at Israel's deliverance. But the best spirits in Israel's public life often noted with sorrow the death and suffering of the enemy armies; and particularly the fact that Israel's soldiers were compelled to inflict that suffering on their foes. In a remarkable speech, made soon after Israel's resounding victory, Mr. Yitzhak Rabin, then Chief of Staff of Israel's armed forces, expressed his sorrow that Israel had been compelled to inflict suffering on the soldiers of the enemy. His words were a precious modern translation of the theology of the ancient folklore which provides the story for this piece. Our legend and echoes of it which we find in modern literature are authentic expressions of an important Jewish ethic, the ethic of compassion. Yes, compassion even for the enemy.

Of course, as already indicated, this ethic is not an easy one. Some might say that it is not only impractical, but that it is even unethical because it seems to deny the proper place of justice and retribution for the wicked. A rabbinic teaching even cautions against showing mercy to the wicked, and warns that whoever does so might end up not only by showing kindness to the evil person, but could also act cruelly to the good person. Justice could be turned upside down and the standards of civilized morality could become unsettled by the absence of a clear division between the good and the bad. The Egyptians were the cruel oppressors of the Hebrews for many generations, and at the end it was God Himself who brought about their punishment. But that is precisely the point made by the legend. It is God alone who is the final arbiter of justice for the wicked, and when that takes place—as it must—even through human agencies, our feelings must be somewhat tempered by the thought that all people are children of the One Creator of all mankind.

Some readers might feel that the midrash leaves us with the modern question of our attitude to the Nazi war criminals who were responsible for the Holocaust. The Jews will never forget the barbaric behavior of those who were involved in the slaughter of one third of the Jewish people. Those who were guilty had to be found, and if convicted had to be punished with all the severity of the law. Ultimately proper standards of justice have to prevail if human society is to exist at all. But there is no rejoicing. On the contrary, there is sadness that human beings could act like savage beasts, and sombre reflections on the slow course of justice.

So, in summary, our midrash about the angels who were prevented from singing at the Reed Sea has nothing at all to say about the primacy of justice and the proper retribution for the wicked. Justice must be done, and evil must be punished—if society is to survive.

The single lesson of the midrash is that all mankind including the wicked are creatures of God. So ideally there should be no rejoicing even at their downfall. Appropriate to the theme is the curious anecdote told of Rabbi Meir and his wife Beruriah. The rabbi had been constantly harassed by hooligan neighbors who were making life for him rather miserable. So he prayed for their death. Beruriah saw what he was doing and quietly criticized him. "Perhaps you think you have biblical support in the verse *Let sinners cease out of the earth, and let the wicked be no more* (Ps. 104:35)," she said. "But remember the verse does not really say *hoteim* "sinners," but *hataim* "sins." So you should rather pray for the end of sins and then there will be no more sinners." Rabbi Meir accepted his wife's comments. He prayed for an end to sin, and sure enough his troublesome neighbors turned over a new leaf and began to behave properly.

46

~

The Lord of History

The people of Sodom and Gomorrah became cruel and arrogant because of their wealth and the lusciousness of their land which they refused to let anyone else enjoy in case the new-comers would remain permanent residents and deprive them of some of their wealth. So with the design to keep strangers away and also to terrify any residents who might show compassion to the poor or the needy traveller, they enacted a number of barbaric laws.

If a poor man passed through the city they would each give him a coin on which the donor first scratched his name. But they prohibited anyone from selling him food. When the poor man died from hunger each one would come back and retrieve his coin. One day a young girl took pity on a poor starving stranger and she gave him some bread which she had hidden. After a few days, when the townsfolk saw that the man was still alive they investigated the matter and discovered the girl who had been feeding the beggar. They arrested her, stripped her naked, covered her body with honey and left her tied up on a roof under the hot sun where she was stung to death by thousands of bees.

Soon after, the townspeople decreed death by burning to anyone who fed even their local poor. One day, two young girls went with their pitchers to get water from the well. One asked the other, "Why do you look so pale today?" The second girl answered, "Because we have no food in the house." Whereupon the first girl went home and filled her pitcher with flour; and secretly they exchanged pitchers.

However, the people found out what she had done in feeding her poor companion; and she was executed.

Pelotit was the name of one of Lot's daughters. Whenever she saw a starving man in the street she took compassion on him and secretly gave him some food. But her courageous charitable actions were soon discovered and she suffered a terrible execution. Before she died, Pelotit cried out to God and asked for justice to be done to the people of Sodom and Gomorrah. After that, the fate of the evil cities was sealed, and the divine verdict of doom and total destruction of the cities was decreed (*Ber. Rab.* 49; *PDRE.* 25).

* * *

These legends are not only elaborations of the biblical text. If that were all, the rabbis did not have to go quite so far in fabricating stories of the social evil and corruption of those cities. What they really wanted to do was to provide an additional dimension to the picture in order to defend the thesis that God is just in his dealings with the world. After all, there was total destruction of those cities, and with the exception of Lot and his family, every human being in them perished. Abraham's pleading with God was to no avail because there were no righteous people there on whose merit the cities might have been saved. The rabbinic folklore now adds stories which illustrate the depravity of the people so that there was no room for divine mercy. God's patience had been stretched to its final limits, and justice demanded the destruction of the cities and their barbaric inhabitants.

Why all this? Because in rabbinic theology God is the Lord of history. So ultimately everything that happens takes place in accordance with the divine rules of justice. It may take a long time, but justice is finally done. "The mills of God grind slow but they grind exceedingly small."

In a significant way the rabbinic folklore presents a very serious view of history. "History is bunk!" sneered a famous American tycoon. Other views are more respectful of history, but nonetheless—in some cases—reduce history to a collection of stories of heroes or a series of unrelated chronological events. Going a little deeper into the philosophy of history, the Greeks developed a cyclic theory by which they describe history as essentially repetitions of the same theme, perhaps on the line of Ecclesiastes, and that there is nothing new under the sun. According to this notion the events in history are essentially repetitions of the same processes of human stupidity and failures leading to no ultimate purpose or meaning, *for all is vanity* (Ecc. 1:2, 14). Against this, the Darwinians in modern times taught that history is the story of the progress of human life on every level. There is a natural law of progress leading towards the survival of the fittest. The Jewish concept also emphasizes an overall progress but the progress is sanctioned and in a sense controlled by God and His law. For in Jewish teaching God is not only the Lord of nature; He is also the Lord of history.

According to this philosophy, history is the arena wherein God's activity in behalf of man is real, and in which His divine purpose and plan for man is being slowly revealed. God is essentially in search of man. This religious view of history is full of meaning, and it is in terms of that meaning that all events in history have to be viewed and interpreted. Now since the Lord of history is a just God, it means that all events in history have to be rooted in a just design. This applies, say, to the biblical record of the plagues in Egypt, as well as to Israel's exile from the promised land. In post-biblical history it is a lesson which is applied to the decline of late medieval Spain and to the destruction of Nazi Germany. The modern historian A. J. Froude wrote, "One lesson, and only one, history may be said to repeat with distinctness: that the world is built somehow on moral foundations; that in the long run, it will be well with the good; in the long run it is ill with the wicked. . . . History is a voice forever sounding across the centuries the laws of right and wrong. Opinions alter, manners change, creeds rise and fall, but the moral law is written on the tablets of eternity. For every false word or unrighteous deed, for cruelty and oppression, for lust and vanity, the price has to be paid at last: not always by the chief offenders, but paid by someone. Justice and truth alone endure and live. Injustice and falsehood may be long-lived, but doomsday comes at last to them, in French revolutions and other terrible ways" (Quoted by Isidor Epstein in *The Faith of Judaism*).

Something of this philosophy of history lies behind the rabbinic elaboration of the Sodom and Gomorrah story. Ultimately the God of justice who is the Lord of history calls all nations to account.

MISCELLANEOUS

47

~

A Doomed Baby is Saved by Prayer

Rabbi Simeon once accompanied some colleagues to a nearby town where a friend was celebrating the circumcision of his new-born babe. During the celebration the happy father served his distinguished guests with vintage wine, and they all had a great time and made merry until a late hour. The visiting guests decided to stay on until morning, except Rabbi Simeon who left for home after blessing father and child. He said to the father, "As you have rejoiced at your son's initiation into the Covenant of Father Abraham, so may you rejoice in bringing him up in a good life with Torah knowledge and a happy marriage."

On his lonely way home Simeon met a stranger. "How is it that you are not afraid to travel alone at this unearthly hour?" the man asked.

"And who may you be?" asked the rabbi.

"I am the Angel of Death" the stranger answered, and smiled unashamedly.

"And what makes you so pleased with yourself?" Simeon asked him.

"I am always amused at the way you people say things about which you know absolutely nothing" said Death.

The rabbi pressed him for more information and the angel informed him, "The child whose circumcision you attended and whom you blessed with the hope that he will live a good long life, is doomed.

See here I have the decree which empowers me to take away his life within thirty days."

The rabbi was very distressed at hearing this and said to the angel, "Show me my decree."

"I don't have one for you," said the Angel of Death. "You are engaged in Torah study every day, and whenever your name comes up, more years are added to your life, so just now I have absolutely no control over your end."

The rabbi took up the point and said, "May it be God's will that just as you have no control over my destiny may you lose control over that innocent child's life." And he prayed for the new-born infant who was spared and who lived on to a ripe old age (*Koh. Rab.* 3:3; *Dev. Rab.* 9:1).

*   *   *

The teacher who is the subject of the above story is Rabbi Simeon ben Halafta. He was unique in many ways, not least of which was his extraordinary interest in the natural sciences. He was a keen observer of plant life, animals and even insects. Rabbinic literature contains a number of fascinating anecdotes about his experiments in botany, veterinary medicine, and on his observations on ant behavior. However, a major part of his teaching belongs to the area of folklore, ethics and theology, and he is therefore sometimes referred to as the teacher of *aggadah*. The above story has been chosen because it seems to open up an important question in theology.

Of course, it is not too difficult to interpret the story along liberal lines, and to rationalize that the "Angel of Death" was just a stranger who overtook the rabbi and gave him the bad news that the infant had suddenly become ill, and that after praying for the child's recovery Simeon returned to his host's house to find that the baby had recovered. In the course of time and through the natural process of transmission the story became exaggerated into a miracle tale.

On the other hand, readers of the story may want to leave it as it is, untouched by rational interpretation. Such people may go along with the poet's affirmation that "There are more things in heaven and earth than are dreamt of in your philosophy." It is reasonable to assume that the rabbinic story-teller believed it to be true. But in either case we have learned to ask ourselves the questions, 'Why was the story told? What is its underlying lesson?'

It seems that the real lesson is the power of prayer. On a simple level the story seems to tell that a good person can actually change the course of events through the strength of his prayer. In that light the story is really an extreme example of the efficacy of prayer, and while men of faith do not necessarily believe that prayer will always exercise such power, they would nevertheless hold firm to the belief that in some mysterious way which is not always understood prayer does bring about important changes in the human condition. Certainly this teaching has an honorable place in classical Judaism. But the entire proposition opens up a number of serious questions.

First, can we believe that any man can have the power to intercede in order to interfere with the natural process of life and death? There is ample skepticism shown even in rabbinic literature to such an idea. Thus a thought provoking teaching has it that there are certain doors in human experience over which not even the greatest can have control. Even an angel would be powerless. These are the keys to rain, birth and the resurrection of the dead. The implication of this is that the ultimate questions of life and death are in God's hands only, and no one can influence those ultimate matters.

A second question. In our story the "decree" sealing the fate of the new-born baby had already been issued. Could it be revoked? If so, that means that God, so to speak, can change His mind. But is this a possibility within the framework of a serious theology of God? What would we do with a biblical text like, *God is not a man that He should lie, neither the son of man that He should repent. When He hath said will He not do it? Or when He hath spoken, will He not make it good?* (Num. 23:19). One or two observations are therefore in order.

There are several different categories of prayer, and here we will touch only on the prayer of petition in which we ask God for His help. In Judaism, God is not only the transcendent Creator and Power of the universe. He is also the God who is near, the immanent God, the God of the individual. Jewish faith is consistently in a God who can be approached by prayer and to whom we can open our hearts. In its literal meaning, Rabbi Simeon's prayer succeeded, and the severe decree was actually annulled through the power of his prayer; how or why we cannot know. The mysteries are God's and accepting this the only road open to man is the path of faith. Along that line of thinking, even when our most sincere prayers of petition seems to go unanswered that is no argument against such a prayer. For what sort of religious faith would that be if prayer was always answered with the press of a button? In any case we cannot know what is ultimately for our good. We see only the present, and even that imperfectly. God alone sees all things and therefore His answer to our prayers can be a divine "No," and that could be for our good. The poet Longfellow said, "I thank you, O God, for my prayers which you have answered, and also for those which you have not answered." That was spoken in a spirit of religious faith, for he saw that the divine "No" could also be for his good; and only God can know that.

But then there is a second goal to petitionary prayer, which is not to bring about a change in God's plan for us, but to bring about a change in ourselves. This is a profound religious and psychological truth which is often forgotten. Whatever the outer or practical result of the prayer might be, it is always answered if the worshipper rises from his prayer a better person, worthy of the boon for which he prayed. We pray not so much to bring God nearer to us, but to raise ourselves nearer to God. This is the great therapeutic value of sincere prayer. In this way, deep prayer is always effective, because whatever the "answer" might be we are strengthened by prayer to be better able to understand and face life's trials with greater confidence. In that sense prayer, deep and sincere prayer, can and actually does bring about important changes. Not necessarily in God's plan, but in our own behavior. It can be the most powerful experience in a man's life.

In our treatment of this story we have considered the sequel where Rabbi Simeon prays for the baby's life. This sequel is found in the first of our sources, *Ecclesiastes Rabbah*. It is not found in the later midrashim. There the story ends with the Angel of Death telling the rabbi that he does not know the span of Simeon's life because the good man's piety could always extend it. There is no reference to Simeon's intercession for the infant, and the inference is that the babe died since its time had arrived.

Now in that case we have a different emphasis altogether. The story does not deal at all with the power of prayer, since prayer is not even mentioned. In this version of the story the lesson is that death will come to everyone who lives; but no one can know the time of his death. This lack of knowledge of his ultimate end is the inescapable destiny of every man. Man does not know when he will die, so he sometimes lives as though he thinks he will live forever. The father of the baby speaks in optimistic terms about his child's future. The wine will last. The child will live. The guests will live and will drink the wine at the grown-up youngster's wedding. But the only certainty in life is its uncertainty.

48

The Couple Who Did Not Divorce

A couple had been married for over ten years, and not having been blessed with children they went to Rabbi Simeon bar Yohai to obtain a divorce. This was in accordance with rabbinic teaching that childlessness after ten years of marriage may be taken as a proper cause for divorce. But the couple really loved each other, and they only went to the rabbi for a divorce since it seemed the right thing to do. The man might remarry and have children; or perhaps the wife would remarry and have children from her second husband.

However, Rabbi Simeon bar Yohai sensed the love of the couple for each other, and he offered them some unusual advice. "I remember that when you were married you made a great feast, with plenty to eat and to drink. Now I suggest that you do the same for your intended divorce. Just as you celebrated your marriage with a banquet, so you should prepare for your divorce with a banquet."

The couple thought that the rabbi's advice was very strange. But they still followed his counsel and they made a "separation feast." At the meal the husband said to the wife, "My dear, as a parting gift to you I offer you the most precious thing in the house. You may take it and go back to your father's house." During the feast, the wife plied her husband with a goodly quantity of drink. He drank it all, and more, with the result that he fell into a deep sleep. Then the wife had some of the servants carry him out of the house to her father's house where he was put to bed. In the morning he woke up to find himself in a strange bed in a strange room.

"Where am I?" he asked.

"You are in my father's house" said the wife.

"And how on earth did I get here?" he wanted to know.

"Well, she answered, "you offered me the most precious thing in the house as a parting gift. 'Take it and go back to your father's house' you said. Now for me you are the most precious thing in the house, so I took you while you slept and had the servants carry you here."

The husband was very moved by what his wife had done. So that very day they went back to Rabbi Simeon who advised them against divorce. He prayed for them, and in due course they were blessed with children (*S.S. Rab.* 1:4).

*   *   *

A charming little story with a 'happy ever after' ending. Yet it illustrates a few serious points on the important subject of love, marriage and divorce. The theme is a major subject in Jewish life and rabbinic law dwells on the subject a great deal. Jewish ethical literature and folklore is also rich in ideas on the topic and is embellished with stories and moralistic sayings on the place of woman, the sanctity of the marriage bond and the centrality of the family.

Our story really touches on two subjects, the matter of divorce and the strength of love between husband and wife. In Jewish law, divorce is relatively easy so long as the legal formalities of rabbinic law are followed. This included an economic safeguard for the wife. The wife cannot be divorced against her will, since the divorce can be effected only by consent of both parties. Only in special cases where one of the parties is unwilling, and the rabbis decide that divorce is morally justified, does the law attempt to break the apparent impasse. Among other factors, the rabbinic law reflects a reaction against the two alien cultures in which Judaism was isolated in the first centuries. These were the pagan Roman civilization on the one hand and the Christian culture on the other. The former was notoriously profligate and a divorce could be given by a husband or a wife without any hesitation or difficulty. In the latter there was no divorce at all, even for the most impossible of marriages. Rabbinic law, based on the Scriptures, seems to stand midway on the issue. The husband alone takes the initiative in instituting a divorce. This does not mean that an innocent wife could not obtain a divorce against a husband unwilling to fulfill his part in the legal proceedings. If there were valid grounds for doing so, then a sympathetic rabbinic court could act in compelling the man to give his wife the divorce she seeks.

If there are no special problems, then divorce in Jewish law is a comparatively simple procedure. Now this does not mean that the marriage bond was regarded as so insubstantial that divorce was a popular feature in Jewish life. The opposite is true. No people in ancient times, and very few in modern times, have made marriage and the family so important. Divorce was the exception rather than the widespread practice. It is true that in the case of the incompatibility of husband and wife, Jewish law provides for relief of the situation by means of a divorce. But this is because of the ideal picture the rabbis had of the marriage union. In Jewish teaching marriage is one of the great religious commands. It is an institution ordained by God and therefore the most natural for man who can find through marriage the fulfillment of all his and her physical, psychological and spiritual potential.

Our story illustrates that childlessness was grounds for divorce. It does not mean that every childless couple divorced after ten years. It simply means that they may—if they so choose—accept their childlessness as a valid cause to terminate the marriage. This is because a central purpose in an ideal marriage partnership is the propagation of children. It is not the only goal, for sure. There are other purposes in marriage which are immensely important. These include mutual love, close companionship and personal human fulfillment. Those values can only be realized in the context of a happy marriage.

This consideration is the second theme of our story which celebrates the quality of true love between husband and wife. Certainly it may not be the romantic kind of love which is often, passionate, sensual and brief. Rather it points to the love which grows cumulatively through years of marriage in which there is mutual understanding and respect. The couple in our story had been married more than a decade but they were still very much in love. The modern pagan concept of 'the seven year itch' is totally alien to the ideal of Jewish marriage. Love before marriage is important; but love after marriage is the true aim for the whole of a mature couple's married life.

49

The Rabbi Who Became an Apostate

Elisha ben Abuya was a scholar who lived in Palestine in the second century. He was the teacher of the illustrious Rabbi Meir who venerated him. This is all the more remarkable since Elisha became an apostate and renounced Judaism. In rabbinic literature he is not usually referred to by his proper name, but by his nickname *Aher* which means "The Other One," that is, the one who became a different person. This was on account of his extreme rebellion against Jewish law and rabbinic teaching. He openly profaned the religious institutions of Judaism and discouraged students from studying Torah.

How did a rabbinic sage come to reject Jewish law and teaching? There are many stories and several theories associated with this question. The most well known is the one which tells that one Sabbath as Elisha was studying near Lake Kinneret, he saw a man climb a tree to take some fledgling birds. He not only took the young, but also took the mother bird with them. This was strictly against Jewish law on two counts. First, the man desecrated the Sabbath. Second, he broke the law in Deuteronomy 22:6, which states that the mother bird must first be sent away before its eggs or chicks are taken, so as to spare the mother additional pain of witnessing the capture of its offspring. However, the bird catcher climbed safely down the ladder and went off with his catch. That same evening, following the Sabbath, Elisha saw a similar occurrence. This time the egg catcher climbed a ladder, and in accordance with the biblical law he first chased away the mother bird before taking its young. But tragedy soon struck the law-abiding man. On his climb down he was bitten by a poisonous snake and was killed. Elisha cried out, "Where is the justice of God who gave the commandment, promising long life to the keeper of the law. Yet He does the opposite, rewarding the one who breaks His law and slaying the one who keeps it.

Another story makes the same point and tells that Elisha, who lived during the martyrdom of the sages in the time of the Hadrianic persecution, saw the tongue of the martyred Hutzpit, the people's translator of the Torah in the mouth of a swine. Elisha was horrified and cried, "How is it possible that the tongue which proclaimed and taught God's Torah should be dragged in the dust?" And he renounced all his former beliefs and lived openly as an apostate (*Koh. Rab.* 7:8).

* * *

The subject of Elisha ben Abuya's apostacy is so appealing that it attracted the attention not only of historians but also of poets and novelists who found the subject fascinating and challenging. In a sense it raises the most troublesome questions not only for Judaism but for all religions which teach the existence of a good and all-powerful God. Why does God allow the righteous to suffer and the wicked to prosper? On a simplistic level one can argue that God is not all-good, or that He is not all-powerful. In either case, evil will exist, because God deliberately permits it or because He cannot prevent it. Some ancient civilizations knew of other theories which attempted to solve the problem of evil, notably the answer given by the Dualists, which sought to show that there was more than one power. There was a god of light and good, and also a god of darkness and evil. The Zoroastrians of Persia had such a teaching which exercised a significant influence in the ancient world.

But Judaism holds to its central belief in the only One God who is omnipotent and all-good. So the problem of the existence of evil is clear. As far as our story goes, it would appear that Elisha became an extreme apostate, an atheist who renounced all his earlier faith in God and His law. Witnessing the existence of injustice and evil in a situation where God had promised the exact opposite, destroyed all his faith. If that could happen, he thought, then there is no God and no justice.

Moving away from the sad story of Elisha ben Abuya we still have to ask what Judaism says with regard to the problem of evil in a world created by God. The subject is the most difficult problem in all theology and Jewish religious literature has many different approaches to the question, from the Book of Job to the Psalms, from the Talmud to the medieval and modern philosophers.

Some of the varied views of Judaism on this subject can be briefly stated. First that the nexus between sin and suffering by which it was once thought that all suffering is a just result of prior sin, was broken—chiefly in the Book of Job. Here was a perfectly righteous man who was unjustly reduced to the most extreme suffering. A solution to the problem had to be looked for elsewhere. The rabbis subsequently developed, again from biblical sources, the theory of *Yisurin shel ahavah*, "chastisements of love," the concept that suffering ennobles and purifies, so that in the result the sufferer is a much better man as a result of his experiences. *Whom God loveth He correcteth* (Prov. 3:12). Precious metal is all the more valuable after it has been refined of its dross. A parent who really loves his child will occasionally rebuke him. Both metaphors are frequent in the Bible. Of course such a theory goes absolutely nowhere in answer to severe or prolonged suffering or early death. So another rabbinic theory holds that all reward and punishment is given in the next world and only after death does a person reap his just reward and merited destiny in accordance with the quality of his life on earth. To this is added the thought that the suffering of the righteous in this world is a sure passport to perfect bliss in the life to come, since through his temporal suffering he has, so to speak, paid off for his inadequacies and redeemed himself, and then he can be blessed with total heavenly joy.

It must be admitted that such "solutions" are hardly satisfactory, and the believer is still left with agonizing questions. Some contemporary writers on the subject offer a version of the kabbalistic theory that at times God, so to speak, deliberately "hides His face." This is another way of saying that God, having created the world and man with free will, permits man-made history to take its natural course. Man is not a puppet to be maneuvered by a divine puppeteer over the stage of history, without freedom to choose, to make good or bad decisions and to mold the shape of his own destiny. Within the context of human freedom and responsibility the innocent individual is often caught up in the maelstrom of historic national decisions, as happens in the catastrophe of a war. In spite of some modern sophisticated elaborations of the mystical theory of the "hidden God" it still fails to answer some basic questions, and the problem of the individual righteous sufferer keeps pushing its way to the forefront. As Sholem Aleichem's Tevye the milkman seems to ask God in his frank and challenging question, "Would it have upset any great cosmic plan of God if Tevye would have been speared so much misery?" Further, in classical Judaism, God is the "God of History" who does not "hide" Himself from the ongoing course of historical events.

So finally, we are thrown back to the foundation stone of all religion—the foundation of faith. If all our doubts could be satisfactorily answered then there would be no challenge and little meaning to religious faith. It is precisely because there are unanswered questions and troublesome doubts that religious faith takes on special significance, providing spiritual strength and powerful support to the one who has won that faith. It is not easy to achieve, particularly in the face of evil. But this is the challenge. Elisha ben Abuya was defeated in the struggle, and for the rest of his years he lived a wretched life, without hope and without faith. On the other hand, countless other people have struggled and prevailed over the existence of evil to emerge even strengthened in their faith, and accordingly have been able to live their lives with direction, with meaning, and with confidence in the ultimate goodness of God. For the man with faith there are no ultimate questions. For the man without faith there are no ultimate answers.

Of all the various approaches to the problem, this appeal to faith seems to be the strongest and the most consistent in Jewish literature. It has an additional practical advantage over all other answers, in that while he may not be able to escape suffering, the believer frequently uses it to some advantage, learning from it, becoming more sensitive to other peoples' suffering, and because of his faith he comes out of his experience a stronger and wiser person.

50

~

The Two-Legged Table

One of the most beloved talmudic characters is the first century Palestinian teacher, Hanina ben Dosa. A great sage, moralist and saint, he is also the central figure in some fascinating rabbinic folklore in which he appears as a miracle worker.

His colleagues would frequently ask him to pray for the sick because they believed that his prayers would find quicker acceptance before the heavenly court.

A good part of the folklore which surrounds him relates to his extreme poverty. He was so poor that his wife did not have the flour with which to bake the Sabbath loaves. In order to avoid embarrassment, she would place some burning wood in the oven so that the smoke would appear, and people would think that she too was baking bread for the Sabbath.

An unkindly neighbor guessed what was happening, and one Friday morning she ran into Hanina's house and cried to his wife, "Your loaves are burning!" and she pulled open the oven door expecting to find the smoldering wood. But lo and behold! the oven was filled with bread.

Realizing that miracles were working for them, the rabbi's good wife approached her husband with a strange request. "Hanina" she said, "all your life you have been studying Torah and are God-fearing and pious. You must have laid up a great reward for both of us in the World to Come. Now wouldn't it be perfectly reasonable to ask God to send us just a little of that reward so that we can enjoy it here and now, rather than that we should have to wait for all of it in the next world?"

Hanina was a kindly and sympathetic man so he agreed. "Yes, perhaps you are right" he said. And Hanina prayed simply but fervently, "Almighty and merciful God and provider! We have been taught and we believe that those who live in accordance with Your holy Torah are remembered by You for good in the life eternal, where they live in the fullness of joy and in eternal bliss. Dear God, if in Your kindness and mercy You have preserved for us a reward in the next world, we know that it will be abundant. Yet here we have so little, that my wife cries out from her poverty. Spare us something from the inheritance which You have laid up for us in the World to Come, so that we can rejoice a little also in this world."

God heard Hanina's prayer and immediately a golden leg of a golden table dropped down from heaven and landed at Hanina's door. The rabbi and his wife were overjoyed and gave thanks and praised God.

But their troubles were not over. Next morning Mrs. Hanina saw that her good husband looked very sad and troubled. "What us the matter, Hanina?" she asked him.

"Last night I had a dream" he answered, "and I saw in my vision that we were already in the Paradise of Eden. We were in the company of the great and righteous men and women of our people, sages and saints, heroes and martyrs. And they were all happily seated around tables which stood securely on three legs. But we were very embarrassed and uncomfortable because our table wobbled on two legs!"

Hanina waited for a response from his wife, and it soon came. "In that case" she said, let us go quickly and pray to God to take back the gift which He gave us yesterday."

Immediately on hearing this, Hanina went into a corner to pray; and his wife also prayed, that God take back His gift. And that is what happened, for the precious gift disappeared when a hand came down from above to take it away. The rabbis add that the retrieval of the gift was a greater miracle than its giving (*Taan.* 24–25).

* * *

Now every mature student of rabbinic literature knows that folklore is not to be read as historical truth—even if the story is in the Talmud. There are different levels of truth, and historical truth is only one kind. There is also moral truth; and the rabbis frequently attempt to teach that kind of truth by a parable.

The question the reader always has to ask is, "What is the purpose of the story?" When Aesop the Greek told his fables, the moral was usually very clear. Not always so with rabbinic folklore. So what can be made of the story of Hanina and his gift which came down from heaven and which he wanted to return?

It is a story which has been variously interpreted and we have a wide choice of meanings. The first and obvious point made by the story touches on the concept of the after-life and God's reward to the righteous in the Hereafter. That doctrine is really not explicit in the Bible and it took many centuries and influences to become a fairly developed belief in mainstream Judaism. By the time of Hanina ben Dosa, the belief in life after death and the doctrine of reward and punishment in the World to Come were established tenets in rabbinic Judaism. The medieval philosophers included these teachings in the principles of Judaism. In Judaism, we only arrive at principles of theological doctrine. We don't begin with them.

As an extension of this, the rabbis wanted to teach that one cannot have the best of both worlds. In other words, you take your reward either in this world or in the next, and that ideally the reward for the righteous is reserved for them in the World to Come. But that notion is difficult to accept, and most certainly it is not borne out by experience in the practical world. In fact we see thankfully, many very good people who do enjoy the fruits of their labor and worth in this world. And why ever not? Poverty and suffering has never been seriously regarded as a Jewish value. Judaism is the "cheery creed."

Then there are the moralists who read the Hanina story as a guide in life that we frequently have to reject the immediate pleasure for the sake of the distant, but greater happiness. A student will give up present pleasures for the sake of the remote good. Parents undertake some sacrifice so that the future of their children will be more secure. A business man will often skimp and save, depriving himself of many desirable things in order to invest his time, energy and resources in what can be a successful future. The present good is often sacrificed for the remote good.

Hanina's story, then, speaks to us in many tongues and with different messages, and every man will learn from it what he wills. Rabbinic folklore can be a great instructor.